Novel Perspectives

WRITING MINILESSONS INSPIRED BY THE CHILDREN IN ADULT FICTION

Shelley Harwayne

HEINEMANN
Portsmouth, NH

Heinemann
A division of Reed Elsevier Inc.
361 Hanover Street
Portsmouth, NH 03801–3912
www.heinemann.com

Offices and agents throughout the world

Library of Congress Cataloging-in-Publication Data
Harwayne, Shelley.
Novel perspectives : writing minilessons inspired by the children in adult fiction / Shelley Harwayne.
p. cm.
Includes bibliographical references.
ISBN 0-325-00877-9 (acid-free paper)
1. English language—Composition and exercises—Study and teaching. 2. Creative writing (Elementary education). 3. Children in literature—Study and teaching. I. Title.
LB1576.H283 2005

2005020869

Editor: Lois Bridges
Production: Patricia Adams
Typesetter: Kim Arney Mulcahy
Cover and interior design: Catherine Hawkes, Cat & Mouse
Cover photograph and interior student portraits: Donnelly Marks
Interior photographs: Artifact photographs in part openers taken by the author from her personal collection
Manufacturing: Louise Richardson

Printed in the United States of America on acid-free paper
09 08 07 06 05 RRD 1 2 3 4 5

for my grandchildren
Andie, Ben, and Will

with great love
and
gratitude

for showing me
the world
through their eyes

Contents

Acknowledgments

I must begin with a sincere thank-you to all the writers whose novels continue to inspire, nourish, and delight us. Educators have rich reading lives to share with their students because of the hard work and brilliance of so many novelists (as well as journalists, poets, playwrights, short story writers, and so on) whose work is stacked high on their night tables. It is my hope that teachers buy multiple copies of the novels noted in this book, form collegial reading groups, and spend hours together rejoicing in the fictional worlds created at the hands of these most talented writers.

Next, I'd like to thank all the friends, colleagues, and family members who emailed titles, clipped book reviews, and telephoned whenever they thought of yet another appropriate novel starring a young child. I am particularly grateful to Hindy List, Maureen Barbieri, and Andrea Lowenkopf, great readers, great teachers of reading, and great teachers of teachers, who seem to have read every great book before most of us have even heard of it. Then, too, I'd like to thank all the conference attendees who handed me titles on little scraps of paper at the end of a workshop. Know that I bought them all.

I am especially grateful to my daughter, J.J. Leitner, and daughter-in-law, Alison Fried, who not only recommended titles but opened their personal libraries to me and allowed me to borrow their books for months on end. How wonderful to be surrounded by young women who not only are gracious, kind, and generous accomplished professionals and wonderful mothers, but also have great taste in books.

I'd also like to pay tribute to all the small bookshop owners, many of whom are fighting to keep their beautiful doors open. It's always rewarding to talk to booksellers who actually read the books they sell and know how to make perfect matches between readers and texts.

In addition, I would like to express gratitude to all the teachers who have welcomed me into their classrooms across the country, allowing me to work with their students and offering feedback on lessons I've shared. None of you has ever left a child behind.

To all my friends at Heinemann, thank you for always being there in so many ways and on so many occasions. You were there for us when we opened the Manhattan New School in September of 1991. You were there for me when I served as superintendent of School District #2 and we had to evacuate and re-create schools in the aftermath of September 11, 2001. You were there for me when I retired from the New York City schools in July of 2003. And of course, you have always been there for me whenever an idea for a new book bubbled up. So thank you to Lesa Scott, president, Leigh Peake, executive editor, Maura Sullivan, associate editorial director, Amy Rowe, editorial assistant, Eric Chalek, marketing copywriter, and copyeditor, Beth Tripp. A very sincere thank-you to Patty Adams, production editor, who brilliantly handled all the details of this book and so graciously respected my grandmother responsibilities along the way. All of your competent and caring hands guarantee that teachers across the country always have powerful professional books to read, discuss, and most important, lead to improved teaching and learning for students.

Then too, a special thanks to cover photographer Donnelly Marks and her assistant Lee Chabowski. Not only did you take beautiful photographs, but you did so with patience and playfulness, as my grandson Ben frolicked in the background.

I especially want to express my heartfelt gratitude to my editor, Lois Bridges, who continues to see more in me than I see in myself. Lois is a brilliant editor, the kind who makes you want to write better books and more important, makes you want to live a more humane and giving life.

I must also pay tribute to all the wonderful educators at the Manhattan New School for continuing the dream. Thank you to Karen Ruzzo and Sharon Hill for their inspired leadership and to all the teachers who work so hard to offer students the finest public education imaginable. A very special thank-you to Barbara Santella, an essential member of the school community, for her behind-the-scenes role in the cover photograph and to the fifth-grade students who grace the cover. A sincere hug of appreciation also goes to Ann Marie Corgill for allowing us to meet in her breathtakingly beautiful classroom.

And finally, my family. To my husband, Neil, thank you for your love, friendship, and guidance. Thank you for encouraging me to join you in retirement, for taking the role of grandfather so seriously and for carrying it out so joyfully, for getaways to the Galápagos, and for making sure all those bookstore bills get paid on time.

To my son, Michael, and his wife, Alison, and to my daughter, J.J., and her husband, David, thank you all for your love, humor, brilliance, and support. And of course, thank you for entrusting me with your children. Being a full-time grandmother began a new chapter in my life, and I take great pride in being part of the lives of Ben Harwayne and Andie and Will Leitner. Young children bring hope to the world and remind educators everywhere that we must continue to close our classroom doors and do what is right for children.

Introduction

Two years ago, on a cross-country flight to Washington state, I filled the hours reading Jodi Picoult's *My Sister's Keeper.* The following day, when I arrived at a school in Seattle to talk to students about their writing, I opened the conversation by referring to the book. In fact, I read aloud an excerpt, suggesting to the fifth graders that if the main character, Anna, had been real, I think she would have been a great participant in the writing workshop. At one point in this compelling family story, Anna talks about the language of childhood. Picoult writes,

> When you are a kid you have your own language, and unlike French or Spanish or whatever you start learning in fourth grade, this one you're born with, and eventually lose. Everyone under the age of seven is fluent in *Ifspeak*; go hang around with someone under three feet tall and you'll see. What if a giant funnel-web spider crawled out of that hole over your head and bit you on the neck? What if the only antidote for venom was locked up in a vault on the top of a mountain? What if you lived through the bite, but could only move your eyelids and blink out an alphabet? It really doesn't matter how far you go; the point is that it's a world of possibility. Kids think with their brains cracked wide open; becoming an adult, I've decided, is only a slow sewing shut. (2004, 299)

This excerpt led to a lively conversation about young people's penchant for "What if . . . ?" questions. (I was quick to point out that their own cracking open of possibilities need not contain venomous insects, violence, or trauma.) The room filled with students' own "What if . . . ?" inquiries, and we talked about how some of them could lead to important topics for students' future writing.

This experience of sharing excerpts from novels I had read with students came to be repeated dozens of times over the last two years. Of course, throughout my teaching career, I have always wanted to serve as a literacy mentor for students, letting them know that I read for pleasure outside of school. But this kind of sharing became more targeted, more purposeful, more connected to my assessed needs of the students as *writers*, not necessarily readers. In fact, that first experience in Seattle began a literary journey for me, one in which I became consciously obsessed with a particular kind of adult novel—the kind in which either the story is told from a young child's point of view, or the author looks back on the grown character's childhood, or the author richly details the experiences of the children who live in the novel.

I am referring here, not to coming-of-age stories, like the *Catcher in the Rye* variety, but mainly to stories that explore even younger children's unique perspectives. Browsing my personal library, I was surprised to discover that I already owned many books that fit this category, although at the time I had not been deliberately collecting them. I then began asking friends, family members, and especially teaching colleagues about the books on their shelves, wondering if teachers are particularly attracted to novels that illuminate the world of the child. This will come as no surprise: they are.

When my first grandson was born, I enrolled in a course in infant CPR that offered suggestions for baby-proofing the child's home. The nurse leading the class suggested we tour our homes on our knees in order to see the world through a toddler's eyes. Teachers, too, need to see the world through their students' eyes, no matter their height. Teachers want so desperately to understand the students in front of them, appreciating their individual ways of viewing the world, acknowledging the very special challenges and problems they face, and admiring their attempts to figure out how this planet and everything on it works.

Novels that focus on the child's world remind us that children are not miniature adults. These novels push us to wonder, Do my students have similar thoughts, concerns, fears, attitudes, interests, pastimes, or quirky behaviors as the children I have come to know at the hands of such accomplished writers? Do I have a student like Katie (on page 12 in Elizabeth Berg's *Durable Goods* [1993]), who tries to dig dimples into her own cheeks? Am I teaching a student like Lark (on page 56 in Faith Sullivan's *The Cape Ann* [1988]), who, while wandering a drugstore, wonders what people do with trusses, sanitary napkins, and enema bags? Is it possible that my students are as curious about language as Evelyn is (on page 2 in Laura Moriarty's *The*

Center of Everything [2003])? She questions the meaning of *Iron Curtain*, unable to imagine how a curtain can be made of metal.

Then, too, as more and more teachers face one-size-fits-all curriculum mandates and prepackaged units of study, these novels raise the question, What will be appropriate for *my* students? It is my hope that this book will remind us to approach each group of students with fresh eyes, getting to know them well as individuals and as a group, before we make decisions about which genres, conventions of print, author studies, research topics, or elements of craft to teach.

This book is a compilation of excerpts from some of my favorite novels, all incorporated into minilessons to be shared with young writers when the need arises. Sharing these passages with students can enrich the writing workshop in many ways. First, many students will respond with, "I have ideas like that! I didn't know I could share those thoughts in writing workshop." For other students, particularly those students who struggle with generating ideas for their writing, hearing these passages read aloud and being encouraged to respond to them will convince students that their own lives are worth writing about. When the writing workshop fills with rich and resonant conversations, students will appreciate that they each have important stories, ideas, experiences, and opinions to share. Above all, it is my hope that these passages will inspire students to be as curious, observant, and insightful as the children in these novels. If teachers are to have any rule in their writing workshops, let it be, "There is no indifference allowed. This room is a passivity-free zone!"

I have included brief introductory remarks for each lesson, merely as suggestions. Of course, my hope is that teachers will discover their own important reasons for sharing these passages, their own ways of powerfully introducing them, as well as their own stories to tell in response to them.

Or the passages can be used in a totally different way. These short passages can easily be turned into overhead projections or duplicated for distribution and marking up. Teachers can then lead class discussions on the quality of the writing, focusing in on different aspects of each author's craft.

Additionally, it is my hope that teachers will be inspired to read the novels cited, perhaps using these titles for staff book clubs. These books are *not* appropriate reads for young children, but they will undoubtedly lead to rich adult conversations. In Jonathan Hull's novel *Losing Julia* (2000), the main character, an elderly man, is saddened to see the popularity of self-help books that take center stage in most bookstores. He asks, "Doesn't anyone realize that the best self-help books are in the literature section?" The wonderful writers quoted in this text did not create novels to enrich our writing workshops. They wrote them to enrich our lives.

It is just an added benefit that when we read for nourishment, pleasure, and to satisfy our own curiosities, along the way we sometimes discover gourmet treats that deserve to be shared with our students. In the reading list at the back of this book, I have placed an asterisk next to those books that are particularly studded with passages to share with young writers. Teachers will, no doubt, find in them additional appealing passages and be able to develop their own accompanying teaching points.

There is no better professional preparation for teachers of literacy than to carve out time to take care of their own reading alongside their own writing. Ultimately, my greatest hope is that teachers will use this text to enrich their writing workshops, as they enrich their own reading lives.

PART ONE

On Discovering Topics

LESSON 1

Using a Writer's Notebook

Sometimes when I am reading a novel for pleasure, away from school and away from all of you, I come across passages that remind me of the kind of writing many of you attempt to do in your writer's notebooks. The passages sound so much like they could have been written by students in this class. They are filled with childhood interests and ideas, the kinds of topics young people write about. They are honest and surprising. And most feel like little snippets of thoughts rather than fully developed stories.

For example, in *Some Things That Stay,* a novel by Sarah Willis, the author gives these words to Tamara, the young main character:

> I used to wish I could paint like my father. With pastels I drew trees and hills and suns, I could draw them all separate, and you'd know exactly what they were, but I couldn't put them together. I could never figure out the depth. It's like music, which I love. When I try to sing, I can get each note, but the notes never slide together, become a melody. I'm good at math. I like taking apart the functions. I like the way things add up to a right or wrong answer. I like the fact that I'm good at it. But sometimes I take out my pastels. Sometimes I wish I could sing. (2002, 2)

Many of you express strong feelings in your writer's notebooks and let one thought lead you to another, making surprising connections like Tamara does here. She moves from drawing to music to math.

In the next passage, Amir, the main character in Khaled Hosseini's *The Kite Runner,* reflects about winter in his city of Kabul. He thinks not about one specific winter but about all winters, as many reflective notebook keepers might. The author writes,

> Winter.
> Here is what I do on the first day of snowfall every year: I step out of the house early in the morning, still in my pajamas, hugging my arms against the chill. I find the driveway, my father's car, the walls, the trees, the rooftops, and the hills buried under a foot of snow. I smile. The sky is seamless and blue, the snow so white my eyes burn. I shovel a handful of the fresh snow into my mouth, listen to the muffled stillness broken only by the cawing of crows. I walk down the front steps, barefoot, and call for Hassan to come out and see.
>
> Winter was every kid's favorite season in Kabul, at least those whose fathers could afford to buy a good iron stove. The reason was simple: They shut down school for the icy season. Winter to me was the end of long division and naming the capital of Bulgaria, and the start of three months of playing cards by the stove with Hassan, free Russian movies on Tuesday mornings at Cinema Park, sweet turnip *qurma* over rice for lunch after a morning of building snowmen . . . (2003, 48)

I wonder if any of you can write a notebook entry that begins with the words, "Here's what I do on . . ."? Those beginning words will probably get you thinking about something you do over and over again, not a one-time event.

Katie, the main character in Elizabeth Berg's *Joy School* (1997), loves to watch ballerinas. The author writes:

> I can't stand straight on ice skates. I wobble and fall a lot. Still, this does not keep me from the main pleasure of it, which is that when I skate, in my head I see ballerinas. I have seen them on television often, and once my mother took me to see them for real. I was young, only six, but I remember every single detail about that day, including that sitting in front of me was a woman wearing one of those stoles where the foxes bite each other's tails, and black round beads are where their eyes used to be. I still do not understand this idea. It seems like whoever made it up was saying, Ho, let's just see how much I can get away with. The sight of that stole made me feel sick in the knees but I just looked around it to watch the ballerinas. I stayed so still watching them I had a crick in my neck later. They

> were so, so beautiful and of another world. That's how it seemed to me . . . (See complete passage on pages 47–48.)

This passage sounds so much like a rich notebook entry as Katie recalls experiences, shares opinions, allows one thought to suggest another, shares pictures in her mind's eye, and moves from the present to the past. If she were a student in our class, this kind of honest writing might lead her to an important writing project.

In another novel by Elizabeth Berg, called *What We Keep,* the young main character, Ginny, reflects on breakfast. Here's what she says:

> I didn't like getting dressed for breakfast; it made the food taste different. I liked not even washing my face or brushing my teeth first, if the truth be told. I liked to be as close to the sleep state as possible, then let the colors and smells and sights of breakfast foods be my wake-up, rather than the rude splash of water. I did this on school days, too—came down and ate breakfast first, then got dressed. (1998, 127)

If Ginny were a real student in our class, I would remind her to save her notebook forever so that she would remember the likes and dislikes of her childhood years. I am so impressed with her thinking. I never thought that food might taste different depending on the clothes you are wearing. I wonder if any one else in the world shares that opinion.

Let's look at another example. In Seamus Deane's *Reading in the Dark* (1996), the main character is an unnamed young boy. At one point in the novel, he talks about going to the circus with his sisters and brothers to see a magician, Mr. Bamboozelem, do a disappearing act. This passage also sounds like the kind of writing many of you hope to do in your writer's notebooks. The author writes:

> From the shadow of the benches, standing against the base of one of the rope-wrapped poles, I watched him in his high boots, top hat, candystriped trousers ballooning over his waist, and a red tailcoat of satin which he flipped up behind him at the applause, so that it seemed he was suddenly on fire, and then, as the black top hat came up again, as though he was suddenly extinguished. He pulled jewels and cards and rings and rabbits out of the air, out of his mouth, his pockets, ears. When everything had stopped disappearing, he smiled at us behind his great moustache, swelled his candystripe belly, tipped his top hat,

> flicked his coat of flame and disappeared in a cloud of smoke and a bang that made us jump a foot in the air. But his moustache remained, smiling the wrong way up in mid-air, where he had been.
>
> Everyone laughed and clapped. Then the moustache disappeared too. Everyone laughed harder. I stole a side-long glance at Eilis and Liam. They were laughing. But were they at all sure of what had happened? Was Mr. Bamboozelem all right? . . . Everyone was laughing and clapping but I felt uneasy. How could they all be so sure? (See complete passage on page 6.)

I can just picture this young boy returning from his circus trip and recording his observations as well as his honest concerns in his writer's notebook. Many of you record special events in your writer's notebooks, and hopefully you are able to do like this young boy and ask important questions of the event.

Books Noted in this Lesson

Some Things That Stay Sarah Willis

The Kite Runner Khaled Hosseini

Joy School Elizabeth Berg

What We Keep Elizabeth Berg

Reading in the Dark Seamus Deane

LESSON 2

Keeping Lists

One way to guarantee that you will always have important topics for writing is to keep a running list in your notebook. You could use the last page to continually jot down topics or ideas that pop into your mind, ones that you will get to someday.

Another way to use lists to generate writing ideas is to think of a particular broad category that appeals to you and make a list of items that connect to this category. For example, in Donna Tartt's book *The Little Friend*, the main character, Harriet, fills her notebook pages with all kinds of lists. The author describes them as follows:

> Lists of books she'd read, and books she wanted to read, and of poems she knew by heart; lists of presents she'd got for birthday and Christmas, and who they were from; lists of places she'd visited (nowhere very exotic) and lists of places she wanted to go (Easter Island, Antarctica, Machu Picchu, Nepal). There were lists of people she admired: Napoleon, and Nathan Bedford Forrest, Genghis Khan and Lawrence of Arabia, Alexander the Great and Harry Houdini and Joan of Arc. (2002, 83)

You can also make lists of ideas, not just items. For example, in Joyce Maynard's novel *The Usual Rules*, the main character, a young girl named Wendy, is being taught by her stepfather to crush pecans with a rolling pin. In order to encourage her to be more forceful, he suggests she think of things she doesn't like. She quickly comes up with the following list:

> People who are cruel to animals, . . . People who litter. People who sit down on the seats on the bus that are supposed to go to handicapped people and senior

> citizens. Mom's boss, that makes her stay late all the time. People who just give you dirty looks when you go into a store with breakable things, just because you are a kid. (2003, 15)

If Wendy were in our writing workshop, I could imagine her recording this list of the things that she finds upsetting in her notebook. Of course, I would then ask her if any of these phrases could lead to some important writing.

In the novel *Hilda and Pearl*, by Alice Mattison, Hilda, one of the main characters, finds a page from her daughter Frances' notebook. The author writes,

> "Ways to Help Mommy and Daddy" she had written at the top. She'd numbered ten lines but had only written down two ways: "1. Help with the dishes. 2. Don't say things that remind them of things." (1995, 281)

You may not want to make a list of ways to help your parents, but you can take lessons from Frances. You might try coming up with your own category, beginning with the words "Ways to . . ." You might also number to ten, and unlike Frances, attempt to complete the ten-thought challenge.

Sometimes reading someone else's list might even give you ideas for creating your own. For example, in Ann Beattie's novel *Picturing Will*, the author lists young Will's fears. Listen to this passage:

> It was interesting to see what a child feared on his own, what fears were communicated to him, and what he was absolutely fearless about. The first time he tasted a soda he had been shocked as if he'd drunk acid. He shrank from cats but would pat any dog. Halloween was a breeze, but as a small child he had not wanted the overhead light to be put off when the Christmas tree lights were turned on. Vampires were shocking but fascinating. Joan Rivers would make him run out of the room. He loved cap pistols but he was afraid of the vacuum. The flamingo night-light was scarier than being left in the dark. Will was afraid to put his face in water but fearless in the seat of a bumper car. He once cried because he looked into a man's mouth and saw gold fillings and thought he could catch them, like a cold. (1989, 42)

I wonder if you can generate a list of things that frightened you when you were younger or those that for some reason continue to frighten you today. Then when you look over the list, you might realize that you have memories, stories, or simply more to say about some of the things you listed.

You could also make a list, as Ann Beattie suggests, of things you are fearless about and fears that you sort of adopted from friends or family members.

Books Noted in this Lesson

The Little Friend Donna Tartt

The Usual Rules Joyce Maynard

Hilda and Pearl Alice Mattison

Picturing Will Ann Beattie

LESSON 3

Recording Childhood Pastimes

Right now, it's easy for you to think that you will remember what it was like when you were a child. Right now, you can't imagine ever forgetting who your friends were, what your school life was like, what your favorite pastimes were, or even what kind of foods you preferred to have in your lunch box. But many years from now, when you've grown older and have gotten busy with so many other things, some of these things will be hard to remember. That's why it is so important to capture on paper your life today and then to hold onto these writings forever. Someday you will be so grateful that you were asked to write and encouraged to save your writing.

In several adult books I have been reading, the fictional children talk honestly about their childhood pastimes, doing the kinds of things that grown-ups tend *not* to do. If these children were real and in our classroom, I would be asking them to record these thoughts in their writer's notebooks. It's possible that some might lead to bigger writing projects and others might remain as important childhood memories.

For example, in Kaye Gibbons' novel *Ellen Foster*, the main character, Ellen, reveals how she amused herself when she was young:

> I had to have something to do so mostly I played catalog. I picked out the little family first and then the house things and the clothes. Sleepwear, evening jackets for the man, pantsuits. I outfitted everybody. The mom, the dad, the cute children. Next they got some camping equipment, a waffle iron, bedroom suits and some toys. When they were set for winter I shopped ahead for the spring. I had

> to use an old catalog but they had no way of knowing they were not in style. I also found the best values. The man worked in a factory and she was a receptionist. They liked to dress up after work. I myself liked the toddlers with the fat faces . . . (1987, 26)

In Rebecca Wells' *Little Altars Everywhere*, Little Shep describes another catalog game, which he plays with his family and friends. The author writes:

> So me and Sidda and Lulu get out the Sears catalog and start cutting it up. We cut up models and things and glue them back together in different ways. It's a old game of ours—you can play it anywhere, because almost everybody has a old Sears catalog laying around the house. I cut off the head of a man modeling underwear and stick it on a power saw. Sidda cuts off a lady's legs and pastes them coming out of a baby's ears. Whoever makes the weirdest things wins. We never get tired of that game. (1992, 72)

In William Lychack's *The Wasp Eater*, the author writes the following about young Daniel:

> In the morning the rain continued. Half asleep, Daniel rolled onto his back and stared at the ceiling and the light fixture. The water stain was a map of the Great Lakes. Or it was the Indian on a nickel. Or a dinosaur fossil. In the ashy light he could blur his eyes and fall back to sleep or else he could turn and watch the evergreen branches sway against the window. (2004, 6–7)

In Jodi Picoult's *My Sister's Keeper*, Anna, the main character, explains how she passes time when she has to wait in the neighborhood laundry:

> I play a game with myself, sometimes, and try to imagine what it would be like to be the person whose clothes are spinning in front of me. If I were washing those carpenter jeans, maybe I'd be a roofer in Phoenix, my arms strong and my back tan. If I had those flowered sheets, I might be on break from Harvard, studying criminal profiling. If I owned that satin cape, I might have season tickets to the ballet. And then I try to picture myself doing any of these things and I can't. (2004, 92)

In Arlene J. Chai's novel *The Last Time I Saw Mother*, the main character, Caridad, returns to her childhood home in the Philippines, a visit that brings back memories she shared with her cousin Mia. The author writes,

> And under those beds lay a different world. We played under them once, amidst the boxes that were stored there. We pretended it was a cave in the mountains where we lived in fear, hiding from the tulisans, bandits that roamed the hills, preying on helpless damsels, just like in the soap operas the laundry woman listened to every afternoon, the radio loud and blaring as she ironed the clothes. So Mia and I rolled on the floor under the bed, inside a cave, not realizing our lives were more in danger from our angry mothers who later found us dirty and sweaty with clothes that had picked up the dust the broom had missed. (1995, 64)

(See also Anna's imaginative game to keep away the night on page 325 in Jodi Picoult's *My Sister's Keeper* and the description of Katie's clothespin dolls on page 91 in Elizabeth Berg's *Durable Goods* [1993].)

Do any of these activities remind you of ones you have made up yourselves? Are there ways that you pass the time that are unique to you? You might consider recording these when you write today. Perhaps some will get you thinking about other important memories, experiences, or events you want to record for the future.

Books Noted in this Lesson

Ellen Foster Kaye Gibbons

Little Altars Everywhere Rebecca Wells

The Wasp Eater William Lychack

My Sister's Keeper Jodi Picoult

The Last Time I Saw Mother Arlene J. Chai

Durable Goods Elizabeth Berg

LESSON 4

Recording Childhood Memories

When you are grown, you will want to remember more than just the games you played as a child. You will want to be able to tell your own children and your grandchildren what the world was like when you were younger.

In Barbara Kingsolver's novel *The Poisonwood Bible*, the young main character, Leah Price, realizes how different living in Africa is from her former home in Georgia, down south in the United States. Leah is impressed with the wonderful plants growing in her family's garden. The author writes:

> And everything that grows: frangipani, jacaranda, *mangwansi* beans, sugarcane, breadfruit, bird of paradise. *Nguba* is peanut (close to what we call them at home, goober peas!); *malala* are the oranges with blood-red juice; *mankondo* are bananas. *Nanasi* is a pineapple, and *nanasi mputu* means "poor man's pineapple": a papaya. All these things grow wild! Our very own backyard resembles the Garden of Eden. I copy down each new word in my school notebook and vow to remember it always, when I am a grown-up American lady with a backyard garden of my own, I shall tell all the world about the lessons I learned in Africa. (1998, 101)

What are the things you vow to remember always? What are the childhood lessons you will want to share when you are grown?

Leah records the precise names of things. You don't have to be living in an exotic place or be studying unusual plants to write with such specificity. What kinds of things will you be writing about that deserve such precision of language and specificity? For example, if you are writing about the pets of your childhood, be sure to include the exact breeds. If you are writing about your favorite family meals, be sure to include the precise names of the foods. If you are recording how you spend your free time, please do not simply say that you read, play games, and watch movies. Years from now when you look back on your writing, you will wish that your information had been more detailed. And if you decide to turn these notebook entries into important writing projects this year, your writing will be more effective, the more particular you are.

Books for this Lesson

The Poisonwood Bible Barbara Kingsolver

LESSON 5

Noting "Aha" Moments

Today, I want to talk about the "aha" moments that happen to us all. When I say "aha," I am referring to those moments when a lightbulb goes off in your mind and you realize that you have figured something out. Sometimes you even realize that what you had been thinking was all wrong, and now you understand. You have it straight. It's as if the truth has made a visit to your mind.

I am reading an adult book titled *Unless*, written by Carol Shields, and I am going to read an excerpt from it aloud to you. In it, the main character is thinking back to when she was a child.

> The moon followed me. When I staggered, seven years old, across the grass in the backyard, my head thrown back, willing myself to be dizzy, I could see how the moon lurched along with my every step, keeping me company as I advanced toward the peony bed. Why, out of all the people in the world, had I been chosen as the moon's companion? What did this mean? Honour, responsibility, blame, which?
>
> I confided to my friend Charlotte this curious business about the moon. But she insisted that, on the contrary, the moon followed her. So back to back, at the end of the lane we paced off steps, she one way, I the other. Immediately I grasped the fact that the moon followed everyone. This insight came mostly as a relief, only slightly tarnished with disappointment. (2002, 100)

Isn't that amazing? She thought when she was seven years old that she had been chosen especially as the moon's friend. Now she realizes that all of us feel like the moon follows us.

In another favorite book of mine, *Durable Goods* (1993), by Elizabeth Berg, the main character, a young girl named Katie, reveals what she used to believe about how radios worked.

> Once, when I was listening to his radio, my father came home. I sat up fast. You weren't supposed to play his radio without asking. But he wasn't mad. He sat down and asked me did I know how a radio worked. I told him that when I was little I thought there were real people in there, swaying before their microphones. There were tiny girls singing in formals, little men in tuxedos, their eyebrows wrinkled from singing like Eddie Fisher. And there were little instruments: saxophones you could fit into matchboxes, pianos no wider than a quarter.
>
> He interrupted me. "You know better than that now, though, don't you?"
>
> "Oh, yes," I said.
>
> "So how do radios work?"
>
> "Well, I . . . I think there are tubes."
>
> "Yes?"
>
> "And some electricity."
>
> "Yes?"
>
> "You have to plug it in."
>
> He laughed. And then he told me how radios worked . . . (See complete passage on page 100.)

Have you ever stopped to think about how some invention or gadget works? Were you surprised when you discovered how it really worked?

In yet another novel, *The Butcher Boy*, by Patrick McCabe, Francie, the main character, is talking with a young friend named Joe. The author writes,

> I could hear a plane droning far away. One time we were standing in the lane behind the houses shading our eyes from the sun and Joe says: Did you see that plane Francie? I said I did. It was a tiny silver bird in the distance. What I want to know is, he said, how do they manage to get a man small enough to fit in? I said I didn't know. I didn't know much about planes in them days. (1993, 2)

Imagine thinking that a very small person had to be the pilot because from far away the plane appeared to be so small!

In *The Secret Life of Bees*, by Sue Monk Kidd, the main character, a young girl named Lily, also admits to a youthful misunderstanding:

> I had the same birthday as the country, which made it even harder to get noticed. When I was little, I thought people were sending up rockets and cherry bombs because of me—hurray, Lily was born! Then reality set in, like it always did. (2002, 21)

(See also Ursula Hegi's *Stones from the River* [1994], page 36, for Trudi's belief that storks bring babies and Leif Enger's *Peace Like a River* [2001], page 182, for Reuben's revelation that film actors speak from a script instead of just talking to each other.)

Have any of you had any experiences in which you thought one thing when you were younger and then began to understand how things really worked? Recording these thoughts, saving your writing, and rereading these pages will, one day in the future, help you remember what you were like when you were a child.

Books Noted in this Lesson

Unless Carol Shields

Durable Goods Elizabeth Berg

The Butcher Boy Patrick McCabe

The Secret Life of Bees Sue Monk Kidd

Stones from the River Ursula Hegi

Peace Like a River Leif Enger

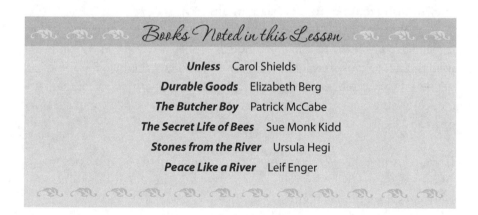

LESSON 6

Letting Objects Spark Thinking

Writers see potential topics everywhere. They notice things in the world and then let their minds follow surprising trails of thinking. For example, Clara, the main character in Alison McGhee's *Shadow Baby* (2000), sees potential topics everywhere. In fact, one day she notices a weathered pot on the side of the road and in an instant begins imagining the life of the pot, weaving a pioneer story to bring that pot to life. Clara thinks . . .

> It may have belonged to a pioneer mother on her way west. Every night she used this pot to cook stew for her pioneer husband and children. Every evening her oldest child scrubbed it out with sand by the creek, and every morning the pioneer mother cooked cornmeal mush in it for breakfast. (See complete story on page 233.)

Clara continues her very compelling story, imagining the cook pot falling off a stack of quilts in the covered wagon. The family searches for it but to no avail, and the family goes hungry that night.

Clara was able to compose such a moving story because she allowed herself to be touched by an object she paid attention to, and then she coupled the object with her knowledge of a historic time period as well as her sense of story.

I wonder how many of us can let ourselves be so moved by objects in our environment that they can take us on a storytelling journey? Can anyone look around the classroom right now and explain how some object got you thinking and spinning a yarn or remembering a true life experience?

Tonight at home, you can challenge yourself in a similar way. Look around your home. Allow yourself to be touched by things that attract your attention. Record your thinking and be ready to share your discoveries, memories, or stories tomorrow.

Books Noted in this Lesson

Shadow Baby Alison McGhee

LESSON 7

Being Inspired at Home

Students sometimes tell me that they run out of ideas for writing, especially in the evenings when they're at home and they don't have their classmates, their teachers, or their class library for inspiration. I think that each of you can become better at letting all kinds of surroundings jog your memories, push you to think new thoughts, fine-tune your powers of observation, or form interesting opinions.

You can be walking down the aisle of the supermarket and discover something you want to say. You can be in the dentist's chair and the same thing can happen. And of course, just hanging out in your home should provide a lot of grist for the mill.

You could look at your old toys or old clothes and be reminded of things you want to say. You can listen to music and capture your response on paper. You can observe the human scene or pet scene and jot down your thinking. Any of these acts, and so many more that take place at home, can help you discover important topics for your writing.

In a book I am reading, one with a most unusual title, *Paddy Clarke Ha Ha Ha*, by Roddy Doyle, Paddy engages in interesting conversations with his parents because he browses the newspaper and is not afraid to ask questions about the articles that catch his eye. The author writes,

> World War Three Looms Near.
>
> I got the paper every day for my da when he'd get home from work, and at the same time on Saturdays. Ma gave me the money; the Evening Press.

> World War Three Looms Near.
>
> —Does Looms mean Coming? I asked my ma.
>
> —I think so, she said.—Why?
>
> —World War Three's coming near, I told her.—Look.
>
> She looked at the headline.
>
> —Oh dear, she said.—That's just newspapers. They exaggerate things.
>
> —Will we be in a war? I asked her.
>
> —No, she said.
>
> —Why not?
>
> —Because there won't be one, she said.
>
> —Were you alive in World War Two? I asked her.
>
> —Yes, she said.—Indeed I was.
>
> She was making dinner; she put on her busy look.
>
> —What was it like?
>
> —It wasn't too bad, she said.—You'd have been disappointed, Patrick. Ireland wasn't really in the war.
>
> —Why not?
>
> —Oh, it's complicated; we just weren't. Your daddy will tell you.
>
> I was waiting for him. He came in the back door.
>
> —Look.
>
> World War Three Looms Near.
>
> He read it.
>
> —World War Three looms near, he said.—Looms, no less.
>
> He didn't seem fussed.
>
> —Have your gun ready, Patrick? he said.
>
> —Ma said there won't be a war, I said.
>
> —She's right.
>
> —Why?
>
> He sometimes liked these questions, and sometimes he didn't. (1993, 24–25)

If Paddy were a student in our class, his concerns about war could be recorded in his writer's notebook.

I hope each of you reads the newspaper at night and is able to talk with someone in your family about what is happening in the world. Sometimes just a photograph will entice you. Sometimes just a headline will catch your eye. Sometimes you will want to read the entire article and follow the story over several days.

Your writer's notebook is a perfect place to record your reactions, questions, concerns, suggestions. Perhaps some of your thinking will be shaped someday into a letter to the editor or a letter to a politician, or your writing will get you started on some important research.

Books Noted in this Lesson

Paddy Clarke Ha Ha Ha Roddy Doyle

LESSON 8

Capturing Ordinary Moments

Young writers sometimes have the idea that only the big moments or very special events in their lives are worth writing about. You need to know that oftentimes the best writing topics come from the seemingly ordinary moments of our lives. These experiences, events, or moments can seem ordinary to other people, but if we write about them well, they become extraordinary.

In Elizabeth Berg's novel *What We Keep*, the narrator, a young girl named Ginny, makes friends with a boy named Wayne. She likes him because he has similar interests and ways of looking at the world. The author writes:

> I recognized in Wayne a kindred spirit. His gaze lingered on the things I found interesting too: A bent-over woman wearing a print kerchief on her head and crossing the street with achy slowness; a shop window with merchandise arranged into the shape of a pyramid; a canvas flap blowing open as it took a corner. (1998, 132)

If Ginny were in our writing class she could explore *why* she found those sights so interesting. If she did, she might uncover an important writing topic.

What does your gaze linger on? Have you written about those everyday things that you find interesting?

Later in the story, Ginny and Wayne notice that the waitress in a restaurant is wearing two different earrings. They don't simply notice this; they try to explore why she might be doing so. The author writes,

> After the waitress left, Wayne and I talked about the earrings, how they didn't match—one was a gold knot, the other a blue rhinestone flower. We wondered

if it could possibly have been intentional; then why that might have been so. "Maybe she wants to get fired," I said. "Maybe her boss is mean." "Maybe she has two personalities," Wayne said. "Two names. Two houses." (133)

When things catch your eye, it's not enough to simply notice them; the real fun comes when you use your writing to explore the meaning attached to these observations.

Books Noted in this Lesson

What We Keep Elizabeth Berg

LESSON 9

Letting Thoughts Flow

Some of you seem to be in a writing rut, stuck in writing narratives alone. In fact, many of your pieces frequently have titles beginning with the words *The Day I* . . . Today, I want to offer you a way to free yourselves from this limited way of writing.

An idea came to me while rereading a very fine novel called *Stones from the River*, by Ursula Hegi. Occasionally, the author shares the honest thinking of the main character, a young girl named Trudi, in a very special way. It's as if the child thinks of a topic that interests her and then jots down a series of ideas connected to the topic.

For example, at one point in the story, the author writes about grandmothers. I can just picture Trudi turning to a clean page in her writer's notebook, writing the word *Grandmothers* across the top, and then recording the following:

> Grandmothers made you finish what was on your plate and told you it was not polite to stare at grown-ups. Grandmothers made you wash behind your ears. Grandmothers could make you do whatever they wanted because they were old. (1994, 40)

I love the way she began each sentence with the word *grandmothers,* and seemed to just jot down whatever came to mind.

At another point in the story, Trudi begins to think about having good manners. The author writes,

> Good manners meant not poking your finger into your nose and not interrupting grown-ups when they talked. Good manners meant offering your seat on

> the streetcar to grown-ups, bending to pick up things that grown-ups dropped, and opening doors for grown-ups . . . (62)

Again, it's as if Trudi just jotted down whatever came to mind connected to having good manners and she began each sentence by repeating the words *Good manners meant . . .*

I think each of you could probably select a broad topic that interests you and do as Trudi has done. Just let your thoughts flow. Don't stop to critique or correct your words. You might also consider beginning each sentence with the same words. I think that might help push your thinking and create a very different kind of writing. Remember, Trudi didn't talk about any one day with her grandmother or any one day when she had good manners. Not everything you write need be a story with a beginning, middle, and ending.

The other thing to keep in mind is Trudi's point of view. The author makes her really sound like a child, sharing the kind of thoughts that children have, not adults. If I were writing about grandmothers or good manners, you would imagine that my thoughts would be very different from a child's. So, whatever topic you select—baseball, baby-sitters, homework—try to tell the truth. Don't try to please grown-ups or sound like a grown-up. Your writing will be strong if you are honest and write from a young person's point of view.

Books Noted in this Lesson

Stones from the River Ursula Hegi

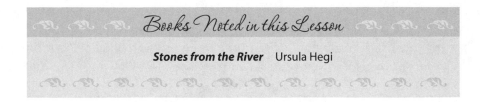

LESSON 10

Noting Views Out the Window

Another wonderful source of inspiration for your writing can come from simply looking out the window—here at school, in your home, at your grandparents' house. Sometimes you see something special, but more likely the view remains the same day after day.

Also, when you are traveling, the passing scenery can inspire you to write. All the more reason to carry your writer's notebook with you at all times. You never know when you'll have the urge to record.

In Linda Ferri's novel *Enchantments*, the young main character is traveling by train with her father outside Paris, France. The author writes:

> In the train I began to write. With my fountain pen and a turquoise ink that I adored I wrote down what I saw from the window—field after field like an enormous patchwork quilt and every so often a group of melancholy cows. After a while my father asked if he could read what I was writing. I handed him the notebook without hesitating, but immediately I was sorry. What if he thought it was all foolishness? When he finished, he looked at me seriously. He'd never looked at me like that—a long look of surprise as well as respect. He said, "Good. I like the way you write, I like the idea of the quilt." I was in seventh heaven. But when I started writing again, the muse was silent, and the fields and woods and rivers of drizzly France didn't inspire me any longer. (2005, 35–36)

Do you agree with her father that describing the field as a patchwork quilt was very effective? Can you imagine being inspired by fields and woods and rivers? What do you suppose she meant when she said, "The muse was silent"? Do any of you have favorite writing instruments, as this girl does?

In Alison McGhee's book *Shadow Baby* (2000), Clara looks out the window of her church as she waits for her mother Tamar to finish choir practice. She observes an old man hanging lanterns in the woods. Here's how she describes the scene:

> That first night, the first time I ever saw the old man, I dragged a folding chair over to that window and stood on it so I could look through the tiny clear piece of patch-glass onto the sloping banks of the Nine Mile Woods. Down below you can see Nine Mile Creek, black and glittery. You would never want to fall onto it even though it's only a few feet deep.
>
> I watched the old man in the woods that night . . . I watched the old man for what seemed like two hours, as long as the choir took to practice. The moonlight turned him into a shadow amongst the trees, until a small flame lit up a few feet from the ground. (See complete passage on page 4.)

Can you imagine watching someone for two hours? What kind of notes would you take in your writer's notebook? What would be an interesting window for you to look through?

(See also Katie's disappointment with the view out her window on page 201 in Elizabeth Berg's *Joy School* [1997].)

Books Noted in this Lesson

Enchantments Linda Ferri
Shadow Baby Alison McGhee
Joy School Elizabeth Berg

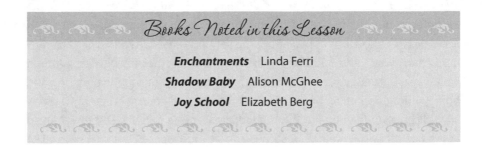

LESSON 11

Responding to Street Scenes

Sometimes on my way to work, I pass a street scene that I wish I could stare at for a long time. I become so interested in someone or something that I would love to just linger there. The sight gets me thinking about so many things and I begin asking myself questions. I feel the need to get more information about the person, the place, or the event that I am witnessing. Has this ever happened to you?

In Donna Tartt's book *The Little Friend* (2002), the main character, a girl named Harriet, has just such an experience whenever she passes the funeral home in her town. The author writes,

> The funeral home—on Main Street, near the Baptist church—was in a tall Victorian house that bristled with turrets and spiky iron crest-work. How many times had Harriet ridden her bicycle by, wondering what went on up in those turrets, behind the cupolas and hooded windows? Occasionally—at night, after a death—a mysterious light wavered in the highest tower behind the stained glass, a light which made her think of an article about mummies she'd seen in an old *National Geographic*. (See complete passage on page 430.)

Harriet has questions about the funeral home; she wonders what goes on in this house with such interesting architecture. I love how she connects the image with the article she read in a magazine. When I read that passage, I wondered if she ever bothered to find out what went on behind those doors or if she really was too frightened to know.

Are there people or buildings or events you see every single day that make you wonder? Are there safe and appropriate ways to get answers to your questions? Your writer's notebook is a perfect place to write what you want to know about your own intriguing scenes. You can also use the pages of your notebook to record the answers to your burning questions.

Books Noted in this Lesson

The Little Friend Donna Tartt

LESSON 12

Learning from Personal Treasures

I am sure that many of you keep personal treasures in your bedroom. Perhaps it is a shoe box that you keep in your closet or under your bed. Perhaps it is a desk drawer filled with very special things, things that you can't seem to throw away, even if your parents can't understand why those treasures are important to you. For some reason these things mean a lot and you think you will never want to discard them.

I was reading a book by a man named Ian McEwan. In his novel *Atonement*, he suggests that the young girl named Briony loved hiding very special items. This passage describes some of her personal treasures:

> ... in a prized varnished cabinet, a secret drawer was opened by pushing against the grain of a cleverly turned dovetail joint, and here she kept a diary locked by a clasp, and a notebook written in a code of her own invention. In a toy safe opened by six secret numbers she stored letters and postcards. An old tin petty cash box was hidden under a removable floorboard beneath her bed. In the box were treasures that dated back four years, to her ninth birthday when she began collecting: a mutant double acorn, fool's gold, a rainmaking spell bought at a funfair, a squirrel's skull as light as a leaf. (2001, 5)

I wonder if any of Briony's treasures remind you of your own. What kinds of things are you holding on to? Can you explain why these items are important to you? Are there stories, strong feelings, or important memories attached to these items? Can you imagine writing about these things or in response to these things in your writer's notebook?

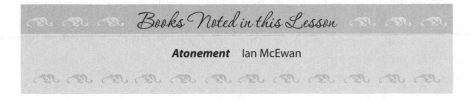

Books Noted in this Lesson

Atonement Ian McEwan

LESSON 13

Overhearing Bits of Conversation

Writers pay attention to all the sights and sounds around them. In fact, sometimes you can get yourself thinking about an important topic simply by overhearing a passing conversation.

In Alice Mattison's novel *Hilda and Pearl*, the young main character, Frances, begins to think about what it means to die when she listens in on some street talk. The author writes:

> One day, when Frances was on her way to Macy's with her mother to buy a coat, she had heard a woman crossing a street in New York say, "Nobody believes he's going to die." When Frances looked into her mind, she discovered it was true of her: although she knew everyone died, she didn't believe *she* would die. She didn't know it in the obvious, ordinary way she knew that she lived on the third floor of an apartment house, the way she knew that if she rang the doorbell, her mother, Hilda Levenson, would open the door. (1995, 7)

It seems to me that fictional Frances has the makings of a writer.

First, she is a good listener. Here she notes the words of a passerby and lets those words push her thinking. I wonder if any of you have ever overheard memorable lines and allowed those words to get you thinking about an important idea.

Next, Frances understands what it means to look into your mind, to probe your thoughts. Do you remember a time when you looked into your mind and made an interesting discovery?

Frances also understands the difference between knowing facts and knowing things in your heart, having instincts about things. Can anyone give an example of something you know based on facts and something you know based on something different—your gut feelings, your intuition, your heart talking to you?

If you were to look over all the writing you have done this year, would you say that most of it is very factual, or is it full of ideas that are based more on your feelings, or is it a combination of both?

Books Noted in this Lesson

Hilda and Pearl Alice Mattison

LESSON 14

Savoring Texts

Your writer's notebook is a perfect place for you to save and savor favorite lines from literature as well as any text in the environment that appeals to you. Once you copy the words down carefully and precisely, you can return to them, figure out their meaning, and figure out why they appealed to you.

In Elizabeth Flock's novel *Me and Emma*, Carrie, the young main character, is taken by a sign in her neighborhood. The author writes,

> Tacked up to the door of the old mill is this: "WARNING: It is unlawful for any person to sell, deliver, or hold or offer for sale any adulterated or misbranded grain. Maximum penalty $100 fine or 60 days imprisonment or both." I copied that down in my notebook from school. (2004, 10)

When I read the passage, I wondered why that sign appealed to the young girl. Did she write it down because she didn't understand the meaning and wanted to ask someone to explain it? Did she write it down because she has a personal or family interest in grains? Did she write it down because she is interested in the law and curious about the business of fines and imprisonment? Has she recorded other warning signs in the community? If so, why?

Have you ever considered recording any signs, advertisements, or headlines in your writer's notebook? Can you explain why they appealed to you?

Are you more likely to record lines from the literature you love? Do you have different reasons for doing so?

Books Noted in this Lesson

Me and Emma Elizabeth Flock

LESSON 15

Jotting Secrets

In *Confessions of an Ugly Stepsister,* author Gregory Maguire writes in regard to the curiosity of Iris, the main character:

> All the secrets of the world are to be discovered and recorded! (1999, 32)

I think this belief can help us generate thoughts for our writer's notebooks. I am not talking here about real secrets you keep with a friend or family secrets that you are told never to share. That's private business. Instead, I'm taking the word *secret* to refer to things you find mysterious, that you want to understand, to unravel so you get to the bottom of things.

Last night I made a list of the secrets of the world I would like to discover and record. In part, my list reads like this:

How can there be so much poverty and wealth at the same time, even on the same block in our city?
How is it possible that sometimes the children of the same parents are so unlike one another?
How can some people learn to speak so many different languages?
Why are some works in the museum considered to be art when to my mind they aren't very different than the works of very young children?

When you face the blank paper today, why not begin by recording the secrets you would like to unravel? Then read over your list of questions and star the one that most demands your attention, that you find most compelling.

How will you go about satisfying your curiosity? How will you use your writer's notebook to answer your question?

Books Noted in this Lesson

Confessions of an Ugly Stepsister Gregory Maguire

LESSON 16

Capturing Visual "Feasts"

I was recently struck by a line in a book I am reading, called *Body and Soul*, by Frank Conroy. In the book, the author describes the young main character's reaction to the first time he walked along a busy city street. He says, "it was a feast." What do you think someone might mean when he describes walking down the street as a feast?

In part, the passage reads:

> He was to walk Third Avenue for many years, until it became so much a part of him he didn't see it anymore. But at first it was a feast. People moving on the sidewalks, automobiles threading through the columns of the el, trucks rumbling in the striated shadows—he drank it in, his eyes leaping from image to image. He would forget to watch where he was going and stumble into a carton of tomatoes outside a fruit and vegetable shop, or bump into a newspaper rack of a candy store as he raised his eyes to watch a train rush overhead. If he fell down and scraped an elbow, it shocked him into remembrance that he was indeed there, that he was physically real . . . (1993, 7)

I suppose the author meant it was a feast for the young boy's eyes because he was so fascinated by all he was seeing.

What are the places that you think of as a feast for your eyes? The next time you witness such a place, remember to capture your visual feast in your writer's notebook. Are there places that have become so much a part of you that you don't see them anymore?

The author also reveals Claude's fascination with very simple acts. In this passage, Claude is watching a shopkeeper take down a box of cornflakes from a high shelf, using a long pole with pincers attached.

> In the store, Claude waited his turn, watching to see if the shopkeeper would use the long pole. Sure enough, someone wanted a box of cornflakes and the old man took the pole, reached up to a shelf near the ceiling, squeezed the grip, and with an astonishing gentleness enclosed the box in the pincers and extracted it. There was a deftness, a precision, to this almost automatic act that Claude found fascinating. (5–6)

Have you ever been so intrigued when watching someone do something as ordinary as taking down a box from a high shelf? If Claude kept a writer's notebook, he could fill his pages with the things that fascinate him. Writers do see the extraordinary in seemingly ordinary things.

(See also page 109 in Elizabeth Berg's novel *What We Keep* [1998]. The main character, Ginny, shares her fascination with observing other people's houses as she rides in a car as well as with observing people at the local Dairy Queen.)

Books Noted in this Lesson

Body and Soul Frank Conroy
What We Keep Elizabeth Berg

LESSON 17

Recalling Family Stories

Each of you probably has a few family stories that you have heard many times. In some families, the stories are told exactly the same way time and again. In other families, the story is told slightly differently each time, depending on who is doing the telling or what kind of mood the teller is in. Most people love to hear family stories, as they remind us of our roots, our traditions, and our heritage.

Writers seem especially tuned to hearing and collecting stories, and not just family ones. They love all kinds of stories because stories remind them of what is important to people the world over and inspire them to create their own.

In many of the adult novels I have been reading recently, the children request stories of their family members or members of the community. For example, Lark, the six-year-old main character in Faith Sullivan's *The Cape Ann*, loves to listen to adults tell stories, especially when she visits the tavern with her grandfather. The author explains that she loved these stories,

> . . . each of which began, "D'ya remember the time . . ." "D'ya remember the time that Mick O'Neill surprised the skunk in the outhouse?" Or "D'ya remember the time that Harriet Good ran back into the burning house to get her teeth? . . ." (See complete passage on page 131).

Do you have any "D'ya remember the time . . ." stories? We probably have a few about our school year together, and each of you probably has a few that are told around your kitchen table at night. Why do you suppose some stories are impossible to forget? Do any of your stories make you think about what is important in your life? Do any remind you of things you need to write about?

What are some of the stories you ask family members to tell over and over again? As you get older, are you understanding oft-told family stories differently? Have any of them led you to do some jotting in your writer's notebook? Have there been times when you wished you had your writer's notebook with you to record what you were hearing?

(See also page 129 in Ann-Marie MacDonald's *The Way the Crow Flies* [2003]. Madeleine, the main character, delights in hearing her father retell the story of a plane crash he survived.

See also pages 42–43 in Pete Hamill's *Snow in August* [1997]. The main character, Michael, loves the Irish folktales his mother shares with him.

Also take a look at pages 7–8 in Seamus Deane's *Reading in the Dark* [1996]. The young narrator enjoyed eavesdropping on his uncles' real-life stories.)

Books Noted in this Lesson

The Cape Ann Faith Sullivan
The Way the Crow Flies Ann-Marie MacDonald
Snow in August Pete Hamill
Reading in the Dark Seamus Deane

LESSON 18

Eavesdropping on Stories

Sometimes I get great ideas for writing picture books by clipping appealing stories from the daily newspaper. I am very fussy about which articles I clip because not every story would be appropriate to turn into a picture book for children. Most of the ones I save are known as human-interest stories or special-feature articles.

For example, in my file is an article about a duck that wandered into a shopping mall. I also clipped an article about a man who is able to twist balloons into incredible sculptures and one about an elderly woman who decided, on a snowy, wintry day, to get out of her wheelchair and make an angel in the snow. I chose these because I think young people would be interested in these topics. Then I take a grain of truth from each article and imagine the pages turning in a picture book. I embellish each story, fictionalizing each one in order to turn it into a meaningful and effective story.

Perhaps I will invent several misadventures for the duck in the mall. The balloon twister in my story might surprise all the neighborhood children on their birthday by creating balloon sculptures just for them. And the elderly woman will do all sorts of surprising things, even though her friends beg her not to.

I discovered that Trudi, the main character in Ursula Hegi's *Stones from the River*, does something similar when she listens to her neighbors talk about one another. She refers to these bits of gossip as secrets and tries to remain unnoticed so she can eavesdrop on the conversations. The author writes:

> If she didn't remind people that she was there, she got to listen to all kinds of secrets. They fascinated her, those secrets, and she hoarded them, repeating

> them to herself before she went to sleep, feeling them stretch and grow into stories- . . . (1994, 72)

And here's another passage:

> Every time Trudi took a story and let it stream through her mind from beginning to end, it grew fuller, richer, feeding on her visions of those people the story belonged to until it left its bed like the river she loved. And it was then that she'd have to tell the story to someone. (73)

In this novel, Trudi doesn't write her stories down. Instead, she tells them over and over to herself, improving them with each telling. When she is ready, she shares them with her friend. Perhaps each of you has a story you have heard or one you have read about in the newspaper that you think you could turn into a wonderful picture book to share with younger children. Then you could read the story aloud to some younger children in our school or learn it so well that you could present it as a storyteller would.

Books Noted in this Lesson

Stones from the River Ursula Hegi

LESSON 19

Writing in Response to Photographs

When you are at home, another wonderful way to generate thoughts for your writing is to browse the pages in your family photo albums or linger on a wall or shelf filled with framed family photographs. Some families also keep a box filled with old and often random photos. These too can lead to interesting questions, discoveries, and topics for your writing. You might even decide to ask relatives when you visit their homes to show you their favorite photos. Pay attention to what catches your eye and record your thoughts and observations.

In Edwidge Danticat's book *Breath, Eyes, Memory*, a young girl named Sophie views a framed family photograph of herself as a baby. She is being held by her aunt, Tante Atie, with her mother at her side. The author writes,

> I moved closer to get a better look at the baby in Tante Atie's arms. I had never seen an infant picture of myself, but somehow I knew that it was me. Who else could it have been? I looked for traces in the child, a feature that was my mother's but still mine too. It was the first time in my life that I noticed that I looked like no one in my family. Not my mother. Not my Tante Atie. I did not look like them when I was a baby and I do not look like them now. (1994, 45)

Isn't it surprising that Sophie had never seen a photo of herself as an infant? The photo also led her to do some big thinking, realizing that she looked like no one in the family.

Do you remember ever looking at a family photo and learning something new? Do you think much about whether or not you look like anyone else?

In Elizabeth Berg's *The Year of Pleasures* (2005), the main character, a woman named Betta, has a ten-year-old friend named Benny. She tells him about her story journal, a file of clipped magazine pictures. She explains that these pictures give her ideas for stories to write. She even asks Benny to make up a story in response to one of the pictures (see pages 165–66).

How different do you think it would be to write in response to magazine pictures rather than to your personal family ones? How different would it be if you chose the magazine pictures that caught your eye rather than if I clipped them for you? Have you ever browsed a magazine and noticed a picture that got you thinking?

(Share also the following scenes of young children interested in family photographs: On page 44 in Donna Tartt's *The Little Friend* [2002], young Harriet spends days poring over family albums, likening the experience to an archeological dig.

On page 130 in Jodi Picoult's *My Sister's Keeper* [2004], young Anna studies the living room gallery of family photographs, calling it a "visual history." On page 252 she thinks big thoughts as she gazes at the framed family photos in her father's office.)

Books Noted in this Lesson

Breath, Eyes, Memory Edwidge Danticat
The Year of Pleasures Elizabeth Berg
The Little Friend Donna Tartt
My Sister's Keeper Jodi Picoult

LESSON 20

Remembering the Songs of Our Lives

Sometimes adults get very good ideas for their writing by thinking of the songs that have been important throughout their lives. I wonder if that is true for children. I wonder if there are songs in your head that you will never forget, even when you grow old.

In Rebecca Wells' novel *Ya-Yas in Bloom*, Sidda recalls her childhood, growing up surrounded by her mother's friends, known as the Ya-Yas. She refers to their group of offspring as the Petites Ya-Ya. In this passage, Sidda thinks about songs the Ya-Yas sang:

> Most of all, I remember the Ya-Yas singing. I remember it from the time I was very young. They sang to us when we were toddlers. They did not sing traditional lullabies. They preferred adapting favorite songs and singing them in combination between torch and choir. I'm sure that the rest of the Petites Ya-Ya, like me, thought that "Smoke Gets in Your Eyes" was a nursery song. And when Mama sang to us about buttoning up our overcoats because "you belong to me," we thought it was our own special going-outside song, composed by our mother for the special occasion of our leaving the house. (2005, 49)

If Sidda were a student in our writing workshop, I'd ask her what other images, memories, experiences, or feelings come to her mind when she recalls the surprising tunes her mother sang to her when she was a child.

Why don't you try to make a time line of the songs that have been important in your life? Then ask yourself why those titles came to mind. Are there images, memories, experiences, or feelings attached to any of your songs? Your notebook is a perfect place to record and reflect on what you come up with.

(Of course, it would be helpful for the teacher to share her or his own timeline of songs and any reflections connected to them.)

Books Noted in this Lesson

Ya-Yas in Bloom Rebecca Wells

PART TWO

On Marveling at the World

LESSON 21

Savoring Moments

I think people who write regularly live their lives a bit differently than people who don't write. Writers pay more attention, observe more closely, question more frequently, respond more deeply, and I think they pause more often, deliberately trying to savor important moments, scenes, or events.

In *The Way the Crow Flies,* by Ann-Marie MacDonald, Madeleine, one of the main characters, is aware of the importance of arriving at her new home. The author writes,

> Madeleine slides from the back seat and turns on the movie camera in her mind—I must remember this, the first walk up to our door. (2003, 39)

Similarly, in Barbara Kingsolver's novel *The Poisonwood Bible,* the young main character, Leah Price, finds herself beginning a new life in the Congo with her missionary family. At one point the author has Leah admit the following:

> I look hard at everything, and blink, as if my two eyes were a Brownie camera taking photographs to carry back. (1998, 102)

I wonder how often that has happened to you? You realize that you want to hold onto certain scenes. Turning on the camera in your mind is a great way to describe this. Turning the camera on will help you remember things. Of course, then writing down your thoughts will guarantee that you will remember important moments.

In *Some Things That Stay*, by Sarah Willis (2000), the young main character, Tamara, also tries to hold onto certain moments of her life. The author writes:

> I try to memorize the way we are sitting, the sky-blue color of my sister's eyes in this light, the way she waves the mosquitoes away with her small little kid's hands, the defiant tone to her voice when she repeats after me, "We'll have to stay." I try to hold inside me the exact length of my brother's hair, the way he sits with his knees bent . . . (See complete passage on pages 269–70.)

Have you ever realized that you wanted to hold onto a moment as it was happening? Have you ever tried to memorize a scene by closing your eyes and trying to see it in your mind's eye? What kinds of scenes have you tried to hold in your mind's eye? Would capturing the scene on paper, in words or pictures, be helpful?

Books Noted in this Lesson

The Way the Crow Flies Ann-Marie MacDonald
The Poisonwood Bible Barbara Kingsolver
Some Things That Stay Sarah Willis

LESSON 22

Using Your Senses

It's not enough for me to simply tell you to add sensory detail to your writing. You can do that well only if you are the kind of person who pays close attention to things in your everyday life, using your senses to appreciate and later recall what those things are like. Then, by carefully selecting the sensory details that evoke the mood you are after, the setting you are trying to create, or the personality you are trying to develop, you will be able to move your audience of readers.

Whenever I come across a young character in the books I read who uses his senses well to understand his world, I think of all of you. Then I slip a bookmark into the page so I will remember to share it with you. I am going to read a few excerpts to you and then talk about what we can learn from these fictional friends.

In Elizabeth Berg's novel *Durable Goods*, the young main character, Katie, decides to turn on her father's radio. Diane is her older sister.

> I am lying on the living room rug, staring at the radio, at the thin red line that finds the station. The radio is a big black rectangle with a long antenna, kept here on the floor, next to my father's chair. I turn it on, hear the loud sound of the baseball announcers. They get so excited. I used to wonder if they were being hit, their surprised "oh!"s sounding just like it. "Oh! Would you look at that! OH!" But they were just watching the game, telling how it was to see it. I turn the dial, get some fancy piano music. I listen with my eyes closed. This kind of music draws pictures in my head, takes me places, acts out whole stories. Diane doesn't like it; she always makes me change the station. But when I grow up I will play it loud in my own house, open the windows wide. (1993, 99)

You really have to look closely to see such detail as the thin red line on a radio band. Have any of you studied something so closely that you could include such specific details? Katie also lets the music inspire her to think new thoughts.

In *The Cape Ann*, by Faith Sullivan, the young main character, Lark, also uses her senses well. When a neighbor offered her a Fig Newton cookie, she explained,

> I didn't like Fig Newtons. They tasted like dried prunes. Also the seeds made it seem like I was eating sand. But I didn't want to make Mrs. Wheeler sad so I ate them and smiled.
>
> Mrs. Wheeler poured herself a cup of tea. I wished she'd put some in my milk. I wasn't fond of milk without something to kill the taste. Mama usually put in a little tea or coffee. (1998, 74)

What a way to describe those cookies! Do any of you have a food that brings strong emotions to mind, that you either adore or detest? Can you describe it in a way that makes us taste it?

In Pat Cunningham Devoto's *Out of the Night That Covers Me*, the young main character, John, is suffering from a very bad sunburn and must rest in bed on the porch for several days. The author describes how he passes the time:

> Nothing up under the tin roof moved without his knowledge. In the morning, after everyone had gone to work, he could hear Aunt Nelda going about her chores, scrubbing out pans, banking the stove fire for later use. He watched dirt daubers as they flew about the business of making mud houses along the cross-beam that ran above the kitchen door. Around eight o'clock every morning, a sparrow came to sit near her abandoned nest situated in the V of crossed boards running to the tin roof. Above him and to the right, an army of ants formed a line, starting over the kitchen door and marching along a beam and down the opposite wall to a point very close to his head, before they disappeared into the porch floor. They seemed to be carrying tiny bits of cornbread. (2001, 77)

When you lie in bed in the early morning or before you fall asleep at night, are there familiar sights and sounds that you pay attention to? How can you get better at doing this?

Caridad, the main character in Arlene J. Chai's novel *The Last Time I Saw Mother*, recalls a shopping trip with her mom. The author writes,

> I was eight years old when I accompanied my mother to a shop run by an old Chinese couple. . . . It was a dark shop with lots of jars and trays inside a long glass counter with sliding doors. The jars contained dried leaves and stalks, seeds and grains, dried flowers and twigs, even black things that looked like the bark of trees. The inside of the shop was warm like an oven and the smell of the strange things hung over it like a cloud that refused to move. (1995, 92)

The author certainly uses sensory details to create a rather mysterious mood. Which details are particularly evocative? What power do the similes have in this passage?

In Dorothy Allison's *Bastard Out of Carolina*, the main character, a young girl called Bone, appreciates visiting the homes of her aunts and uncles. The author writes:

> Over at Aunt Alma's we could listen to Garvey and Grey fight, to Little Earle giggle and squeak, to Uncle Wade drink and cuss, to the radio playing and the chickens clucking outside the windows. Over there we got to slide around on a big tarp with the sprinkler shooting cold water up in a shower. At Aunt Ruth's we could watch Uncle Travis cut up potatoes for her, a beer at his side and a cigarette dangling from one side of his mouth, ashes occasionally dropping into the peels. Aunt Ruth even let us play in just our panties, though after Reese got ringworm Mama insisted we keep our clothes on, and after we got chiggers she made us scrub down as soon as we came home. Reese and I didn't mind. We still wanted to go visiting at every chance. It was alive over at the aunts' houses, warm, always humming with voices and laughter and children running around. (1992, 80)

This passage brims with sensory detail. How many of our senses does the author put to work? I also think this passage demonstrates what it means to capture a place on paper. By carefully choosing telling details, presenting things that happen time and again, and showing the people there in action, the author really helps us understand the setting.

(See also the following sensory passages:

Lark's sensory response to her grandmother's home on page 262 in Faith Sullivan's *The Cape Ann* [1988]

Kate's description of the neighborhood laundry center on page 91 in Jodi Picoult's *My Sister's Keeper* [2004]

Madeleine's description of her new classroom on page 141 in Ann-Marie MacDonald's *The Way the Crow Flies* [2003] as well as her description of the park on page 335

Harriet's description of a dinner meal and how a taste brought back memories of nursery school on page 155 in Donna Tartt's novel *The Little Friend* [2002], as well as page 438, on which the sound of a church bell brings back other early memories

Tamara's thinking in response to the smell of hot tar on page 42 in Sarah Willis' *Some Things That Stay* [2000])

Books Noted in this Lesson

Durable Goods Elizabeth Berg
The Cape Ann Faith Sullivan
Out of the Night That Covers Me Pat Cunningham Devoto
The Last Time I Saw Mother Arlene J. Chai
Bastard Out of Carolina Dorothy Allison
My Sister's Keeper Jodi Picoult
The Way the Crow Flies Ann-Marie MacDonald
The Little Friend Donna Tartt
Some Things That Stay Sarah Willis

LESSON 23

Learning to Look

Throughout the novel *Confessions of an Ugly Stepsister*, author Gregory Maguire provides advice for young artists. He stresses the importance of learning to look. In fact, he notes, "Children, like artists, like to look"(1999, 366).

The author reminds his readers that children are usually very good at paying attention to detail. He describes Iris as she studies a bowl in the wealthy van den Meer home:

> Look at the bowl on the polished table. A bowl from the Orient, van den Meer has told her. But it's not just one thing, a bowl. Look at all the effects that make it up: Deepest in, a lace of purple-gray hairline fractures. Covered by an eggshell wash, through which blue painted lines form blowsy chrysanthemum blossoms. The flowers are suspended in some thin distance of—for lack of a better word—shine. Inside the curve of the bowl, a reflection: a distorted Iris, too blurred to be perceived as ugly . . . (See complete passage on page 79.)

Sharla, a young girl in Elizabeth Berg's novel *What We Keep*, is surprised when her friend wins a prize for drawing a shoe. Her sister Ginny, however, is *not* surprised. The author writes,

> All you had to do was really look at a shoe to see how much was there: the valleys in the creases of the leather, the graceful lines of the hanging laces, the implied history of the absent wearer. (1998, 146–47)

It seems there is a major difference between looking and really seeing. Writers, like artists, have to get good at really seeing. We can practice together in class, by all gazing at the same object and perfecting our abilities to see more and finding just the right words to describe what we are seeing.

Let's all take a look at __________ (e.g., a potted geranium, a class globe, a well-worn backpack) and then jot down what we see. (You can ask students to look at any interesting object, but preferably one that is large enough to be seen by all.)

When describing the object, try to do as these young girls have done. Choose your words carefully. In fact, in *Confessions of an Ugly Stepsister*, Gregory Maguire provides some additional advice. He notes:

> Don't approach something to draw as if you know what it is; approach it as if you've never experienced it before. Apprehend it by surprise. Startle it into liveliness. (1999, 304)

We can substitute the word *describe* for the word *draw* and challenge ourselves to look at our object as if we've never seen one before. Can you each use words to startle our object into liveliness?

Books Noted in this Lesson

Confessions of an Ugly Stepsister Gregory Maguire

What We Keep Elizabeth Berg

LESSON 24

Finding the World Fascinating

Sometimes when I read about young people who find the world a fascinating place, I am struck by the language they use to describe their ways of looking at the world. For example, in Emma Richler's novel *Sister Crazy*, the narrator is a young girl named Jemima. At one point in the story she is holding her mother's hands. The author writes,

> I take Mum's hand at the foot of the stairs and it's the best grip in the world. It's loose, not too loose, firm not tight. She has long fingers and incredibly silky skin and the temperature is just right, cool not cold, and the feel is dry not rough, never rough. I take in all these details about her hands and the way she holds mine because I am not crazy for holding hands . . . (2001, 51–52)

I love her expression "I take in all these details." When in your life have you been conscious of taking in all the details?

At another time, Jem is watching her six-year-old brother, Gus, eat a great quantity of hot dogs stuffed with cheese. Jem says:

> . . . I can easily eat two, sometimes three curly dogs with cheese. So can Gus, which is quite surprising seeing as he is very thin and only six. Gus eats slowly and with great concentration and graceful manners. I have never seen so much food go into such a small human being, and I watch him with furtive fascination and wonder if it will always be like that with him. (85)

"Furtive fascination" implies that Jem is a bit secretive about her interest in her brother's eating habits. Are there things you look at with furtive fascination?

In another episode, when watching the *The Wizard of Oz* with her family, Jem is struck by a comment made by her mother. She says:

> After the film, we sat around for a few minutes and Dad kept singing the Lollipop Guild song and shaking with mirth, and Mum said when she first saw *The Wizard of Oz* she didn't want to be Dorothy but Glinda the Good Witch of the North, played by Billie Burke.
>
> Very interesting. I made a note of this. (60–61)

I am not sure if Jem made a note on paper or just made a mental note, but I think whenever you find something interesting, you too could be saying, "I need to make a note of this."

Books Noted in this Lesson

Sister Crazy Emma Richler

LESSON 25

Asking Questions

I want to talk to you today about how important asking questions is to writers. When I walk down the street with my friends who take their writing seriously, they are always asking questions. Writers are curious about things and always eager to find answers to their questions. If we pass a dog, they might ask the owner, "What breed of dog is that?" If we pass a big apartment building with a water tank on the top, they might ask, "How do you suppose that water tank works?" If we pass a woman feeding bread crumbs to a flock of pigeons, they might ask, "How do you suppose she got started doing that? Do you think she does it every day? What do you think the neighbors think about her?"

Being inquisitive is not just for grown-ups, but for children as well. In fact, very young children often ask so many questions that they sometimes tire their parents out. Unfortunately, as children grow up, they sometimes stop asking so many questions. To be a good writer, you must return to that inquisitive preschool stage.

In Arlene J. Chai's novel *The Last Time I Saw Mother*, the main character, Caridad, admits to never having given up her favorite question, Why? The author writes:

> "Why?" is a word children learn early in life. It was a word I used often as a child. And it was a word I continued to use long after most children had moved on to other words.
>
> The word itself creates an empty sensation. Try saying it now. "Why?" Notice how your tongue touches nothing when you form the word with your mouth. Feel the gap, the space inside your mouth, that it creates. The air. It is a place that needs filling. It is missing an answer. (1995, 56)

Of course, Why? is not the only question that writers ask. They ask many different types of questions because they know how important information is to their readers.

You need to be filling yourself up with the kind of information that interests you so that when the need arises to weave specificity into your writing, you will have a well to draw upon.

I have read several books recently in which the children are not afraid to ask questions. I am going to share some passages with you to demonstrate this curiosity and hopefully inspire you to be wide awake in the world, hungry for information.

For example, in Jodi Picoult's novel *My Sister's Keeper*, Anna visits a pawnshop to sell her locket. Here's how she describes the experience:

> Pawnshops may be full of junk, but they're also a breeding ground for stories, if you ask me, not that you did. What happened to make a person trade in the Never Before Worn Diamond Solitaire? Who needed money so badly they'd sell a teddy bear missing an eye? As I walk up to the counter, I wonder if someone will look at the locket I'm about to give up, and ask these same questions. (2004, 8)

Anna doesn't just notice things, she probes her observations, looking for stories. Your writer's notebook is a perfect place to write what you want to know about your own intriguing scenes. Then, too, you can use the pages of your notebook to record the answers to your burning questions.

In Ann-Marie MacDonald's book *The Way the Crow Flies*, eight-year-old Madeleine, one of the main characters, is concerned about moving into a new neighborhood. This passage describes what went on in Madeleine's head as her family drove toward their new home:

> At the corner of Columbia and St. Lawrence Avenue is a two-tone tan house with an orange VW in the driveway. A plump girl with curly hair is Hula Hooping on the front lawn. As they turn right down St. Lawrence, Madeleine wonders, will I ever Hula Hoop with that girl? Will I get to drive in her van? Or is she moving away? (2003, 38)

Madeleine's dad is in the Canadian Air Force, so the family will be living on a military base. Their area, where families with children live, which is known as PMQ, stands for Permanent Married Quarters. Here's another interesting passage:

> A purple house ahead on the left catches her eye because PMQ driveways are not usually full of old cars and washing-machine parts, or big German shepherd dogs that are not tied up. Who lives there? Scary people? That would be too unusual. (38)

At school, the author reveals Madeleine's attitude toward mathematics. When the teacher is handing out math textbooks, Madeleine even asks questions about the word problems the teacher assigns. Unfortunately, she doesn't ask the kinds of questions that will help her solve the problems. Rather, her questions demonstrate her curiosity about people's lives. No doubt, she will do well in her writing class.

> "Into how many sets of 8 can you divide 120 children for square dancing?" What children? Where do they live? Are they orphans? "At the rifle range Bob scored 267 points. His father scored 423 points. . . ." Who is Bob? Why is he allowed to have a gun? (143)

Sometimes Madeleine speaks the language of childhood, the "Ifspeak" described in the introduction to this book. She is nervous when her father visits the house of an unusual neighbor and asks many "What if . . . ?" questions. See page 72 in *The Way the Crow Flies*.

(See also Tamara's question about growing tomatoes on page 148 in Sarah Willis' *Some Things That Stay* [2001] and Katie's wondering about how pleated skirts kept those "permanent dents" on page 89 in Elizabeth Berg's *Durable Goods* [1993].)

Books Noted in this Lesson

The Last Time I Saw Mother Arlene J. Chai
My Sister's Keeper Jodi Picoult
The Way the Crow Flies Ann-Marie MacDonald
Some Things That Stay Sarah Willis
Durable Goods Elizabeth Berg

LESSON 26

Having Areas of Expertise

People who take their writing seriously understand the value of having an area of interest apart from their writing. Being an expert at something helps you appreciate the importance of specific and accurate bits of information, of precise language, of close observation, of sensory detail. It's no surprise that the word *author* is in the word *authority*. Studying something deeply helps you feel like an authority and helps you appreciate what it means to write with authority. In addition, becoming a passionate student of ballet, karate, gardening, or basketball, for example, can also lead to important topics for writing.

If the following young characters were in my class, you can be sure I would encourage them to keep up their obsessions and possibly refer to them when choosing writing topics. For example, Astrid, a young girl in Janet Fitch's *White Oleander*, meets a young boy named Davey in her new foster family. Davey is very knowledgeable about nature and eager to teach others. Fitch writes,

> The biggest boy, the one with glasses, stood up. "We're catching lizards, you want to?"
>
> They trapped the lizards with shoebox snares down in the wash. The patience of such small boys as they waited, silent, still, for a green lizard to enter the trap. They pulled the string and the box fell down. The biggest boy slid a sheet of cardboard under the box and turned it over, and the middle one grabbed the tiny living thing and put it in the glass jar.
>
> "What do you do with them?" I asked.
>
> The boy with the glasses looked at me in surprise. "We study them, of course."

> The lizard in the jar did push-ups, then grew very still. Isolated, you could see how perfect it was, every small scale, its rows of etched toenails. Made special by virtue of its imprisonment. Above us the mountain loomed, a solemn presence. I found if I looked at it a certain way, I could feel its huge shouldered mass moving toward me, green polka dots of sage clinging to its flanks. A puff of breeze came up. A bird screamed. The chaparral gave off a hot fresh smell.
>
> . . . The biggest boy was suddenly beside me. "Careful of the rattlesnakes. They like those rocks."
>
> I moved away from the rock.
>
> "The western diamondback is the largest of the American vipers," he said. "But they rarely strike above the ankle. Just watch where you're going, and don't climb on the rocks, or if you do, watch where you put your hands. Do like this." He took a small rock and knocked it on the nearest boulder, as if knocking on a door. "They'll avoid you if they can. Also look out for scorpions. Shake your shoes before you put them on, especially outside." (1999, 46–47)

Davey is a great observer of the natural world and if he were a writer, he could take that talent and apply it to all he sees. He also delights in having precise information, another element of good writing.

Do you consider yourself an expert in any subject apart from what you study in school? Has this expertise led to any writing projects?

In Philip Roth's novel *The Plot Against America*, the young boy named Philip is very interested in stamp collecting. The author writes,

> (The small magnifying glass—along with an album for twenty-five hundred stamps, a stamp tweezers, a perforation gauge, gummed stamp hinges, and a black rubber dish called a watermark detector—had been a gift from my parents for my seventh birthday. For an additional ten cents they'd also bought me a small book of ninety-odd pages called *The Stamp Collector's Handbook*, where, under "How to Start a Stamp Collection," I'd read with fascination this sentence: "Old business files or private correspondence often contain stamps of discontinued issues which are of great value, so if you have any friends living in old houses who have accumulated material of this sort in their attics, try to obtain their old stamped envelopes and wrappers." We didn't have an attic, none of our friends living in flats and apartments had attics . . .) (2004, 21–22)

Studying something deeply certainly opens a world of specialized vocabulary. I had never heard of a watermark detector or a perforation gauge. Do any of you have a hobby or area of interest that is marked by unique words or expressions? If Philip were writing about stamp collecting, including those words would prove that stamp collecting is his turf.

In Donna Tartt's novel *The Little Friend* (2002), the main character, Harriet, was very interested in dinosaurs during her childhood. Listen to this excerpt:

> She had from the time she was small, a preoccupation with archeology: with Indian mounds, ruined cities, buried things. This had begun with an interest in dinosaurs which had turned into something else. What interested Harriet, it became apparent as soon as she was old enough to articulate it, were not the dinosaurs themselves—the long-lashed brontosauruses of Saturday cartoons, who allowed themselves to be ridden, or meekly bent their necks as a playground slide for children—nor even the screaming tyrannosaurs and pterodactyls of nightmare. What interested her was that they no longer existed. (See complete passage on page 37.)

Harriet goes on to ask hard questions about dinosaurs, a very important thing for writers to do. How many of you are jotting down questions in your writer's notebook, things you wonder about your areas of interest?

(See also Clara's expertise with tulips on pages 94–96 in Gregory Maguire's *Confessions of an Ugly Stepsister* [1999]).

Books Noted in this Lesson

White Oleander Janet Fitch

The Plot Against America Philip Roth

The Little Friend Donna Tartt

Confessions of an Ugly Stepsister Gregory Maguire

LESSON 27

Paying Close Attention to People

Writers always think about including specific and significant details in their writing. This is especially true when they are trying to make the people on their pages come alive. They try to notice the tiniest things that other people might not notice, carefully selecting those details that will help the reader really get to know each person in the writing.

And even when writers make up a person, crafting fiction, they work hard to include these same kinds of details, ones that will help the reader believe in the character on the page.

Part of becoming a good writer, then, is to study people, to try to notice the small things that say a whole lot about a person. At one point in Gregory Maguire's *Confessions of an Ugly Stepsister,* young Iris is thinking about her mother, Margarethe, and the author asks, "If Iris were to paint Margarethe, what would she notice?" (1999, 157).

That's a question we all can be asking ourselves when we are trying to capture a person or even a place or object on paper. If we were painting it, what distinctive features would we notice and be sure to include in our painting?

I have come across several fictional characters who are quite good at noticing telling details about people. For instance, in Elizabeth Berg's novel *Joy School* (1997), the main character, Katie, pays very close attention to her favorite teacher, Mrs. Brady. Here's how she describes this teacher:

> She has a beehive hairdo, and when she stands by the window, you can see through it. It sort of looks like brown cotton candy. Once I saw a hairpin coming out a little and that is what reminded me that her hair isn't always like that. She has black cat-eye glasses, and she always wears this outfit: a pleated skirt, a

> blouse with usually a round collar, a cardigan sweater, brown shoes with heels so little that you don't know they're heels until she turns around to write on the blackboard. Her handwriting is so clear and beautiful. I can't believe a person does it. Even on the board, every letter so perfect, every line so straight . . . (See complete description on pages 9–10.)

Which lines let you know that the character Katie is especially observant?

In Dorothy Allison's novel *Cavedweller*, young Cissy meets Granddaddy Byrd for the very first time and notices something unusual about his right hand. The author writes,

> Something strange there. The long, skinny fingers with the swollen knuckles lay precisely against each other, ending in an even line. Cissy flattened her own hand against her thigh and immediately saw the difference. Her middle finger extended more than a quarter of an inch past the two on either side of it. On Granddaddy Byrd's right hand the fingers were the same length all across, the nails of the middle three flush with the nail of the pinkie. In each he was missing at least the length of one joint.
>
> Cissy looked up at his face. He was looking right back at her. She flushed with embarrassment . . . (1998, 47)

I wonder if most people would notice the grandfather's unusual hand or if Cissy is particularly observant? I appreciate how she figured out what was different by looking at her own hand.

Similarly, in Roddy Doyle's *Paddy Clarke Ha Ha Ha*, Paddy is a ten-year-old boy who pays close attention to his mother's reading habits. Listen to this passage:

> My ma read books. Mostly at night. She licked her finger when she was coming to the end of her page, then she turned the page; she pulled the corner up with her wet finger. In the mornings I found her book marker, a bit of newspaper, in the book and I counted back to the number of pages she'd read the night before. The record was forty-two. (1993, 61)

I love that Paddy talks about an event that happens over and over, not simply a one-time occurrence. I wonder if anyone else in Paddy's family noticed how his mom read. If he were in our writing class, I think I would ask him why he is interested in his mother's reading habits.

In another novel, *A Complicated Kindness*, by Miriam Toews, the main character, a girl named Nomi, talks about her mother. The author writes:

> There were other things you may not necessarily know or remember about my mother. She liked to pat her stomach, especially if she was standing in the middle of the kitchen staring at the cupboards trying to mentally prepare herself for plunging into some tedious domestic task.
>
> Often when she said the word *yes*, in response to a question, she'd spread her arms out like a symphony conductor calling for a big sound from his musicians.
>
> She liked a made bed.
>
> She had an uncanny ability to predict the weather.
>
> She'd snap towels viciously before folding them, often very close to our heads as we sat watching tv.
>
> She didn't believe in waiting for two hours after eating before going for a swim. "Do fish get out of the water after they've eaten?"
>
> She drove too fast and whenever she parked she'd inch closer and closer to the wall or barricade in front of her until the hood of the car bumped against it. She called it Montreal parking. She'd never been to Montreal but she liked to say *Montreal* whenever she could so that everything, parking, hairstyles, sandwiches, were all, according to her, Montreal-*style*.
>
> She believed in one-hundred-percent cotton. "It wrinkles badly but at least it breathes." (2004, 18–19)

You wouldn't notice such small, quirky things unless you really paid attention. You might try in your writer's notebook to capture a person you know well by doing some close observation and then recording what stands out for you.

(See also Ginny's observation of her sister eating pancakes on page 92 in Elizabeth Berg's *What We Keep* [1998], her observation of her sister's homework habits on pages 119–120, as well as her description of her father's predictable routines on page 186.)

Books Noted in this Lesson

Confessions of an Ugly Stepsister Gregory Maguire

Joy School Elizabeth Berg

Cavedweller Dorothy Allison

Paddy Clarke Ha Ha Ha Roddy Doyle

A Complicated Kindness Miriam Toews

What We Keep Elizabeth Berg

LESSON 28

Figuring Out How Things Work

Writers are curious. They are always wondering about the things that attract their attention. They are always trying to figure out how things work. Sometimes, they don't simply ask questions of experts or look things up in an encyclopedia or on the Internet. Instead, they roll up their sleeves and do some firsthand investigating.

In Frank Conroy's novel *Body and Soul*, for example, the main character, a young boy named Claude, becomes curious about the small white piano in his apartment. The author describes how Claude satisfied his curiosity:

> One day as he sat fooling with a single note—playing it loud, then as soft as he could, then somewhere in the middle—he suddenly wondered what was inside the piano. He got up and examined the instrument. He cleared the stacks of old newspapers, trip cards, and magazines from atop the case, opened the hinge lid, and looked down. An impression of density, and of order. The strings angled down toward darkness. He reached in and turned first one wooden latch and then another, barely catching the mirrored front of the case as it surprised him by falling away. Now he could see the felt hammers, the pins, the levers, and tiny leather strips of the action.
>
> He returned to the bench and played the single note again, watching the hammer fly forward to strike the string. Moving up until his nose was almost touching the mechanism, he pressed the key again and again, trying to understand the forces at work between the key and the hammer . . . (1993, 14)

Do you think understanding how the piano worked might have had an influence on Claude's piano playing? Are there items in your home you would love to take apart in order to understand how they work?

In another book, called *Nobody's Fool*, by Richard Russo, a little boy named Will was playing with his breakfast cereal. The author writes,

> Will was ready. He'd finished his cereal and was engaged in a scientific experiment with the few remaining Cheerios in his bowl. In the beginning, they floated. You could hold a Cheerio under the surface of milk for a long time, but as soon as you removed the spoon, it floated right to the top. You could break it in half, and then the two halves floated. Break the two halves in half and all four floated. But when you broke them into smaller pieces, they bloated up, lost their buoyancy, turned to brown muck in the bottom of the bowl. Without arriving at any conclusions as to what this phenomenon might mean, Will nevertheless found it interesting. It was nice to be able to think such thoughts in peace. (1993, 380)

Have you had any similar experiences? What kind of thoughts roam through your mind when you have such peaceful moments?

In Elizabeth Berg's novel *What We Keep* (1998), young Ginny reveals her passion for taking things apart. Berg describes a summer filled with such experiences.

> I cracked open rocks with my father's hammer. Rubbed gently the damp surfaces I found in various pods I pulled from trees, ripped apart buds for the tight sight of embryonic flowers. I used a pearl-handled steak knife to saw open the high heels of a pair of party shoes my mother was throwing out, and on one brave day when no one else was home, unscrewed the back of the kitchen radio. (See complete passage on pages 20–21.)

Have you ever wondered so much about how something worked that you had to investigate it?

In the writing that you are now doing, are there things you don't know enough about that you need to take time to understand better? If so, why not roll up your sleeves and do some firsthand investigating.

Books Noted in this Lesson

Body and Soul	Frank Conroy
Nobody's Fool	Richard Russo
What We Keep	Elizabeth Berg

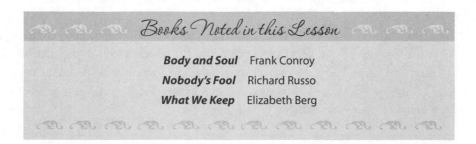

LESSON 29

Learning from Alert Mentors

Sometimes when I am reading a novel, I meet fictional characters who are so alert and imaginative that I wish they were real and could serve as mentors to us in our writing workshop.

In Trezza Azzopardi's novel *The Hiding Place*, for instance, a young girl named Dolores is just such a character. In this scene, she is listening to her mother warn her father about eating raw bacon, or rashers, as it is called in the story. The author writes:

> Worms! warns my mother, when she sees him stretching the rasher between fist and mouth. You'll have a tapeworm inside you six foot long!
>
> I don't know what a tapeworm looks like. I picture the coiled spool of measuring tape in my mother's sewing-box, slithering over the faces of the men from *True Crime*; imagine it inching up my father's throat like a creamy yellow snake. Maybe it's this that gives him heartburn. (2000, 111)

There are so many things to appreciate in this short passage. I appreciate that Dolores listens to family conversations and can recall her mother's exact words. Dolores pictures things in her mind's eye and uses her imagination to bring these things to life.

Dolores connects the tapeworm to a tape measure, playing with language so well. Dolores chooses her verbs so precisely when she speaks—*slithering* and *inching* are such perfect choices. She uses similes to make her meaning clear. I can just picture that creamy yellow snake. She also tries to make things add up, guessing that the tapeworm is causing her father's heartburn.

In Kate Atkinson's *Behind the Scenes at the Museum,* young Ruby also reveals a rich imaginative life. Listen to how she describes the falling snow:

> The curtains in the living-room have been left open and outside I can see the snow falling silently. There are great flakes, like goose feathers, and small, curled ones like swansdown and great flurries as if a flock of stormy petrels had shaken their feathers out. As I watch, the sky fills with clouds of snow feathers from every kind of bird there ever was and even some that only exist in the imagination, like the bluebirds that fly over the rainbow. Most of the Christmas tree needles are on the floor by now but I switch on the tree lights anyway. Then I start spinning the glass balls on the tree. If I work hard at it I can get them all spinning at the same time. Sometimes they bang together and dislodge glitter which falls in a shower of fairy dust all over me. (1995, 170)

Imagine thinking about snowflakes as different kinds of feathers. Both of them sail through the air so gently. I also love the way she calls the glitter fairy dust. The author has given Ruby a most poetic and imaginative voice.

Have you come across any characters in the books you've read that you think would make fine writers if they were real? Be prepared to explain your choices.

Books Noted in this Lesson

The Hiding Place Trezza Azzopardi

Behind the Scenes at the Museum Kate Atkinson

LESSON 30

Appreciating Stories

I often wish that the school day were longer so that we had more time to talk. I especially wish that we had more time to make up stories, the way some grown-ups do for their children at bedtime. I don't even mean that we should necessarily write down the stories we make up. No, I think there is much to be learned from becoming a storyteller, from composing stories out loud. I think we would learn a lot about how stories work and what keeps an audience interested, how to build suspense and how to create an ending that satisfies the listener.

We probably won't be able to carve out enough time at school, but I wonder if there are opportunities for you to make up stories *outside* of school. Perhaps you can do this when you have play dates, baby-sit for younger children, or even as part of your own bedtime rituals.

I recently marked a few passages in some of my favorite adult novels in which the children find ways to weave storytelling into their everyday lives. In *Child of My Heart*, by Alice McDermott, teenage Theresa is spending time with her young cousin Daisy. (Daisy has several brothers and a mean-spirited sister named Bernadette.) They stop at a candy store and Theresa buys one hundred lollipops. When they return home, Theresa makes up a story to tantalize her other cousins. The author writes,

> When we got back to the house, we dumped all of them over her brothers and Bernadette, who were lying on the living room floor watching their allotted hour of television before dinner. The lollipops in their wrappers were wet with snow, some were muddy from where we had dropped them on the walk home.

> "Where did you get these?" Bernadette asked, and before Daisy could answer, I said, "We found a lollipop tree. You should have come." The boys said, "Yeah, sure," but Bernadette couldn't resist grilling us on the particulars, her eyes narrowed, her thin mouth opened skeptically, showing the little blowfish teeth.
>
> A house on the boulevard, I said. A willow tree. A huge willow tree filled with lollipops for the taking. The tree belongs to an old couple, I said, whose only child, a little boy, had dreamed of a lollipop tree in his front yard on the night he died, fifty years ago this very day.
>
> Once a year and only on this day, I said, they make his dream come true by filling their willow tree with lollipops. (And the odd thing is, I said, it was snowing in his dream, too, and it snows every year on this date the minute the old couple hangs the last lollipop on the tree.) They invite children from miles around. I'm surprised you never heard about it before. The old couple serves hot chocolate out on their lawn while the children collect lollipops from the tree. They hire tall men to help lift the smaller children high into the branches. The single rule is that you can pick only as many lollipops as you can carry home—no paper bags or suitcases, oh, and the picking lasts for just one hour, . . . (2002, 10–11)

What a story Theresa has told! The boy cousins actually believe it. What do you think makes the story so convincing? What can we learn from Theresa's storytelling that could help us when we write?

In Kate Atkinson's *Behind the Scenes at the Museum*, young Ruby entertains her teddy bear by retelling stories she has heard as well as inventing original ones. She is unhappily staying with relatives and would love to return to her own family. So it is not surprising that all her stories are about rescue. Here's how she describes her stories:

> I comfort Teddy by telling him stories, stories that involve a lot of rescuing—Rapunzel, Snow White, Sleeping Beauty, detailed episodes of Robinhood in which I am Maid Marion, Teddy is Alan-a-Dale and Auntie Bas is the Sheriff of Nottingham. Or sometimes I am the Lone Ranger and Teddy does his passable imitation of Jay Silverheels. Sometimes we are captives on a pirate ship, already teetering on the gangplank as Sinbad's ship hoves into view; sometimes we are stranded in log cabins . . . (1995, 110)

It makes sense that children would choose stories that help them deal with problems they are facing. Do you know of any fairy tales that connect to your life? Can you explain your choice? Do you know any fairy tales well enough to retell them?

In Dorothy Allison's novel *Bastard Out of Carolina*, the mama shares with her children what it was like to grow up very poor and hungry. She explains the food stories that she and her siblings used to tell, and then her own children do likewise. The author writes:

> "We used to pass the plates around the table, eight plates for eight kids, pretending there was food gonna come off the stove to fill those plates, talking about food we'd never seen just heard about or imagined, making up stories about what we'd cook if we could. Earle liked the idea of parboiled puppies. Your aunt Ruth always talked about frogs' tongues with dewberries. Beau wanted fried rutabagas, and Nevil cried for steamed daffodils. But Raylene won the prize with her recipe for sugar-glazed turtle meat with poison greens and hot piss dressing."
>
> After awhile Reese and I started making up our own pretend meals. "Peanut butter and Jell-O. Mashed bug meat with pickles." Mama made us laugh with her imitations of her brothers and sisters fighting over the most disgusting meals they could dream up. (1992, 72–73)

Have your parents shared any storytelling pastimes from their childhoods, ones that you have tried yourself? Why do you suppose children seem to enjoy talking about nauseating combinations of foods like these?

(See also Iris as a storyteller on page 101 in Gregory Maguire's *Confessions of an Ugly Stepsister* [1999], and Lark's dramatic play called *The Lady Caller* on pages 49–51 in Faith Sullivan's novel *The Cape Ann* [1988].)

Books Noted in this Lesson

Child of My Heart Alice McDermott

Behind the Scenes at the Museum Kate Atkinson

Bastard Out of Carolina Dorothy Allison

Confessions of an Ugly Stepsister Gregory Maguire

The Cape Ann Faith Sullivan

LESSON 31

Solving Mysteries

It makes sense that people who pay close attention to what is happening around them would be good at solving mysteries. After all, detectives must notice the tiniest details, search for additional clues, play their hunches, eliminate possibilities, notice patterns of behavior, and make things add up.

In two novels that I have been reading, the young main characters are interested in being like the literary detectives they admire, solving mysteries of their own. For instance, in Rebecca Wells' *Ya-Yas in Bloom*, Sidda looks back on her childhood. The author writes,

> As I sat on the couch with the rest of the kids, watching TV, I heard something that I thought I better check out. I was deep into a Nancy Drew phase. Every single thing that occurred—a car on the gravel road, Willetta claiming someone stole her favorite pot for cooking starch, a creak in the floorboards—presented itself as a mystery begging for me, only me, to solve. I tiptoed backward out of the den—girl detective, hoping no one would follow. (2005, 53)

Have you ever been in a "Nancy Drew phase," when small mysteries called out to you to be solved? How might such a phase support your writing? What are some recent concerns that you felt obliged to check out? Have you considered writing about any of these concerns?

Jemima, the young narrator in Emma Richler's novel *Sister Crazy* (2001), has the wild idea that her mother could be a witch. The author explains what she does about this hunch:

> With my homework stuff is my Mummy casebook. In Sherlock Holmes there is always a casebook and I am making a case. I have a list of observations, only one

per page, leaving space for special remarks and so on. (See complete passage on page 54.)

Have any of you ever made a case in your writer's notebook? In other words, have you ever had a hunch and tried to prove your thinking by gathering facts and making careful observations? Sherlock Holmes solved crime mysteries, but you don't need a crime to create a casebook. You just need to want to prove a point. Perhaps some of you have a writing project that lends itself to the term *casebook*.

Books Noted in this Lesson

Ya-Yas in Bloom Rebecca Wells

Sister Crazy Emma Richler

PART THREE

On Revising Writing

LESSON 32

Thinking New Thoughts

I think we don't talk enough about how important it is to try to think new thoughts when we write. Writers don't want to say the same things that other people have already said. They want to share original thinking and they also work hard to choose just the right words and arrangements of words so that their thoughts are conveyed in fresh and surprising ways.

I am reading a book called *The Center of Everything* by Laura Moriarty. The main character, Evelyn, talks about what she is learning from her teacher at school. The author writes,

> Ms. Fairchild says people used to think the Earth was flat, with an edge you could fall off of. They thought the sky was just a big dome, and that the sun moved across it every day, pulled by a man with a chariot. It's easy to look back now and say, "Oh, you dummies," but when I'm up on the roof, watching the sun disappear behind the fields on the other side of the highway, I can see how they would think of that. If everybody I ever met told me that the Earth was flat and that somebody pulled the sun across the sky with a chariot and nobody told me anything else, I would have believed them. Or, if no one would have told me anything and I had to come up with an idea myself, I would have thought that the sun went into a giant slot in the Earth at night, like bread into a toaster. (2003, 11)

Isn't that a striking way to explain how the Sun goes down at night if you had never been taught about Earth's rotation? How clever to imagine the Sun going into a slot in Earth, like bread into a toaster.

(It's possible that some children have only had experience with toaster ovens and have never seen an "old-fashioned" toaster that pops up slices of bread. This description, therefore, may need clarification. You might also want to talk about why "Oh, you dummies" is not an acceptable way to talk and also warn children about the dangers of sitting on rooftops.)

At another point in the story, Evelyn is commenting on a difficult neighbor, Mrs. Rowley, who has a pet poodle named Jackie O. Listen to this passage:

> . . . she does not say hello, but just stands there, watching me like she is a frog and I am a fly and if I get too close to her, that's it. She will not let me pet Jackie O because she says Jackie has a nervous condition that I will only aggravate. But I think Mrs. Rowley is the one with the nervous condition. She leans her head over their balcony sometimes and says, "Please don't jump rope on the pavement because I can hear the *skip, skip, skip*, and it's very annoying."
>
> I tell my mother when Mrs. Rowley was little, someone must have told her if you don't have something nice to say, don't say anything at all, only she got confused, got it backwards. Only talk if you are going to say something mean. (See complete passage on page 15.)

Evelyn is a great observer of people and she has quite a way with words. That frog-and-fly image really helps me understand how Mrs. Rowley looks at Evelyn. Most of all, I appreciate Evelyn's original thinking. She thought of that old saying, "If you can't say anything nice, don't say anything at all," and decided that her neighbor learned it in reverse. How clever! She really makes the point of how distasteful she thinks Mrs. Rowley is.

Ginny, the main character in Elizabeth Berg's *What We Keep* (1998), sneaks into the house next door on the night that her neighbor has moved away. As she tours the house, she sensitively describes the loneliness that she feels. The author writes:

> The dining room missed its lace tablecloth and the turkey dinners Mrs. O'Donnell had served when her husband was alive. The kitchen tap dripped, looking for macaroni to rinse . . . (See complete passage on page 35.)

I love that she thought about the things that remained and imagined that they had feelings. I don't know if anyone else has ever had a similar way of thinking about an empty house.

In Sue Monk Kidd's book *The Secret Life of Bees*, a young girl named Lily is interested in the names of a group of sisters she moves in with. They are named

May, June, April, and August. August explains that when she and her sisters were children, they each were given special privileges during the month they were named after. Fewer chores, more favorite foods, more staying up late. Lily is fascinated with this concept, as this passage shows:

> After hearing this, I'd spent a good amount of time trying to think up which month I would have liked to have been named after. I picked October, as it is a golden month with better-than-average weather, and my initials would be O. O. for October Owens, which would make an interesting monogram. I pictured myself eating three-tiered chocolate cake for breakfast throughout the entire month, staying up an hour after bedtime writing high-caliber stories and poems. (2002, 137)

Lily certainly offers surprising reasons for selecting October. She also helps us picture her special treat by including such specific details as "three-tiered chocolate cake for breakfast." And of course I just love that she would stay up late writing high-quality stories and poems.

I wonder how many of you have examples in your writing folders or notebooks in which you have recorded some original thinking. If you do, please mark those pages and bring them to our share time.

And if you don't think you have ever done any original thinking in your writing, perhaps this is the right time to challenge yourself. Why not begin your writing time by rereading your old writing to see if you have some fresh thinking to add to previous work? Or, if you are about to begin some new writing, try to do some fresh thinking as you write.

(See also Katie's thoughts about time on pages 41 and 75 in Elizabeth Berg's *Durable Goods* [1993].)

Books Noted in this Lesson

The Center of Everything Laura Moriarty
What We Keep Elizabeth Berg
The Secret Life of Bees Sue Monk Kidd
Durable Goods Elizabeth Berg

LESSON 33

Enriching Narratives

Many of you are writing narratives about important events that you shared with your families. I recently came across a passage in the novel *Stones from the River*, by Ursula Hegi, that I think may help many of you enrich those stories. The author describes the pleasure young Trudi takes in eavesdropping on her father when he talks to customers in his tobacco and book shop (called a pay-library). At this point in the story, the men in their village have just returned from the war. The author writes,

> Hidden on the footstool behind the counter of the pay-library, enveloped in the lavish scent of tobaccos, Trudi would soak in the words that her father chose to tell the men about the town during their absence. His arc of vision was higher than hers, wider, and though he spoke of events that she, too, had witnessed, they took on a richer texture and became richer still afterwards, alone—she fused them with her own observations. (1994, 29)

In other words, Trudi appreciates hearing her father talk about an event that she has seen as well. I love her expression "soak in the words."

She appreciates that her father tells the story differently, perhaps having a different viewpoint, including different details, highlighting different moments, even coming to different conclusions. And then she realizes that when she retells the story in her own mind, she weaves in her father's thinking with her own, creating an even better story.

I wonder if your stories would grow richer if you did the same. Why not ask your family to share memories of the events you are trying to capture on paper? Listen carefully to what they say. Perhaps they will jog your memories, present new ways of recalling the experience or add thoughts that hadn't occurred to you. You can then choose to weave those new words, images, or ideas into your writing.

Books Noted in this Lesson

Stones from the River Ursula Hegi

LESSON 34

Strengthening Letters

All the qualities of good writing that we think about when we compose narratives, poems, picture books, or even informational texts also apply when we write letters. Good writing is good writing.

In Elizabeth Berg's novel *What We Keep* (1998, 118), the parents have created a ritual called Correspondence Day, when the children have to write letters to family members. Ginny, the main character, struggles to write a letter to her grandparents because she doesn't believe that she has anything new and interesting to say. She has grown tired of writing the same old thing, the standard greeting followed by what she had for dinner and ending with an untrue but expected statement about looking forward to school. It's no wonder she is facing writer's block. She is writing anybody's words instead of sharing what is really on her mind.

Do any of you write to family members on a regular basis? What kinds of information do you share?

In *Crow Lake*, by Mary Lawson (2002), the young main character, Kate, began to write regularly to her Aunt Annie after her parents passed away and her brothers, Luke and Matt, became her caregivers. Many years later, after her Aunt Annie has died, Kate gets those letters back. Many are written in invented spelling, as she was very young when she wrote them. This excerpt begins with two of those letters:

Sunday 11th October

Dear Aunt Annie,

How are you? I hope you are well. We are all well. Bo is well. Miss Carrington came. Mrs. Mitchell came she brot stew. Mrs. Stanovich came she brot pie.

Love, Kate

Sunday 18th October

Dear Aunt Annie,

How are you? I hope you are well. We are all well. Mrs. Stanovich came she brot a chicken. Mrs. Tadworth cam she brot ham.

Love, Kate

I have those letters now. Aunt Annie died a year ago of cancer, and after her death Uncle William sent them to me. I was touched that she had kept them, particularly given their remarkably consistent lack of style and content. There was a whole box of them, covering a period of several years, and when I read through the early ones, I thought, good God, they say absolutely *nothing*. Looking through them again though, trying to imagine Aunt Annie reading them, picturing her unfolding the ragged scraps of paper, adjusting her spectacles and peering at my scrawl, I realized that if she looked hard—and she would have looked hard—she probably found a certain amount of comfort between the lines.

For a start she would have known that we were not starving and that we had not been forgotten by the community. She would have known that I was in good enough shape to sit down and write a letter and that Luke and Matt were organized enough to see that I did. The fact that I invariably wrote on a Sunday implied that we had a routine, and Aunt Annie was of the school which set great store by routines. And every now and then there would be a scrap of genuine news . . . (See complete passage on pages 134–35)

At first, Katie is so critical of her letters. Do you know what she means by lacking in style and content? Then, looking back on them more carefully, she is able to read a lot into them. She demonstrates that it can be important to write to loved ones even when we don't produce powerful writing.

Imagine if she had known how to write high-quality letters when she was younger. How do you think those letters would have been different?

Books Noted in this Lesson

What We Keep Elizabeth Berg

Crow Lake Mary Lawson

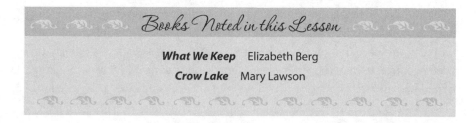

LESSON 35

Learning from Feedback

We spend a lot of time in our writing workshop sharing our writing and asking for feedback from one another. I think sometimes we are too polite, always quick to say, "I really like your story!" I think we need to be much more honest but tactful at the same time. In other words, we must be able to ask honest questions and seek clarification without being afraid of hurting one another's feelings. All of you must take on the role of writing teacher, learning to ask questions and make suggestions graciously.

In Khaled Hosseini's novel *The Kite Runner* (2003), the main character, Amir, is reading to his friend Hassan, a child who does not know how to read (see page 30). Instead of reading from the book in his hands, Amir decides to make up his own story. The story is so well received that Amir decides to write an original one that very night. He composes a story about a man whose tears could turn into pearls and make him rich. In the end, the man becomes so greedy that he kills his own wife so that his tears will make him even richer. Amir shares his story first with a family friend who is very complimentary, especially about Amir's ability to create irony in his first story. He also receives feedback from his friend Hassan after reading the story aloud to him. Hassan has a question. The author writes,

> "Well," he said, "if I may ask, why did the man kill his wife? In fact, why did he ever have to feel sad to shed tears? Couldn't he have just smelled an onion?"
>
> I was stunned. That particular point, so obvious it was utterly stupid, hadn't even occurred to me. I moved my lips soundlessly. It appeared that on the same night I had learned about one of writing's objectives, irony, I would also be intro-

> duced to one of its pitfalls: the Plot Hole. Taught by Hassan, of all people. Hassan who couldn't read and had never written a single word in his entire life . . . (See complete passages on pages 31–34)

Hassan was a splendid conference partner, responding honestly and kindly to Amir's story. And by doing so, he taught his friend a great deal.

What do you think Amir's family friend found ironic? Have you ever read or written anything that contained irony?

If you were going to warn one of your classmates about the concept of a plot hole, how would you describe it?

Books Noted in this Lesson

The Kite Runner Khaled Hosseini

LESSON 36

Learning to Pause and Rewind

Many of you choose to write narrative accounts of events that have been important to you. Many of you would be having an easier time capturing these events on paper if you had kept your writer's notebooks handy during the experiences. In other words, if you had jotted down the details, the emotions and the actual words that were spoken as you welcomed your new baby sibling home, or won a Little League game, or rode on a roller coaster for the very first time, it would be a lot easier to weave those thoughts into your narrative today. Instead, many of you have to think long and hard about what the experience was like. Sometimes it helps to talk to people who were with you in order to jog your memory. Sometimes it helps to look at photographs from the day. Sometimes you even have to invent things that you can't recall.

I recently came across a passage in a novel I was reading, called *The Usual Rules*, by Joyce Maynard, that I think may suggest yet another way to help you recall experiences that you want to capture on paper. In this passage, the narrator is talking about a young child named Louie.

> *Pause,* Louie liked to say when he got up from the couch to go to the bathroom or get a cookie and he didn't want you to do anything until he returned. *Rewind,* he said when he came running back in the room and it looked like things had been going on without him. Sometimes, they'd be watching a video, but he also said it if someone was reading to him, or if they were playing Go Fish or checkers. He thought you could freeze time in real life, same as on a video. (2003, 20)

Wouldn't it be amazing if we could really freeze moments in time? It might help those of you trying to recall an experience to ask yourself, "For what moments during that experience would I have wanted to press the pause button, freezing those moments in time? What would I see if I were to press the rewind button?"

You might even ask these questions of friends and family members who shared the experience with you: "What moments deserve to be frozen in time? What comes to mind when you rewind the tape?"

Books Noted in this Lesson

The Usual Rules Joyce Maynard

LESSON 37

Adding Believability

Some of you have been trying to write realistic fiction and have been running into trouble because your stories are not believable. One suggestion I have for you is to attempt to act out your stories, to take on the role of the characters and try to imagine what they would most likely say and do in response to the situations you have created.

In a novel I am reading titled *Hilda and Pearl* by Alice Mattison, the main character, Frances, is making up a story with her friend Lydia. They decide to use props to help propel the story. Lydia's mother asks the girls what they are doing. The author writes:

> "It's for school," Lydia said. "We're making up a story about nurses for school, and we're using the dolls to help us make up the story." As far as Frances knew, Lydia was not planning to make up a story until she said that, but now Frances said it would be easy to write a story about the dolls—about nurses and their boyfriends, that is—and they began planning the story as well as playing the game. (1995, 104)

Do you think props could help you act out your stories? Could you enact them without the use of props? Do you think using dolls could actually have gotten in the girls' way, making the playing more important than the writing?

Do you think playing with your favorite toys could help you come up with fresh ideas for writing realistic fiction? Do you think collaborating makes writing easier or harder?

(See also page 32 in the *The Kite Runner*, by Khaled Hosseini [2003]. The main character, Amir, recalls playing with a turtle with his childhood friend Hassan. Their play led them to create a most adventurous story.)

Books Noted in this Lesson

Hilda and Pearl Alice Mattison
The Kite Runner Khaled Hosseini

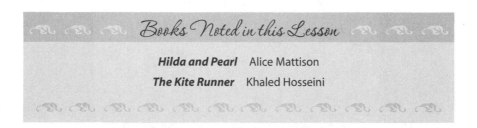

LESSON 38

Observing and Reflecting

Many of you have gotten quite good at capturing scenes on paper. Your pages are filled with detailed observations. Today I want you to think about taking that kind of writing a step further. Instead of just recording your observations, I want you to let the reader know what you think about the things you are witnessing. And I don't mean simply adding a sentence or two beginning with "This scene makes me feel . . ." No, I am referring here to subtly weaving in your responses to your observations. The following excerpts from literature will illustrate my point.

In Sarah Willis' novel *Some Things That Stay*, the main character, Tamara, is observing her neighbor through her bedroom window. I can just picture her jotting the following thoughts in her writer's notebook.

> The thin, tangle-haired girl puts down her basket and runs over to the tire swing. The tire is tied by a rope to the thick limb of a twisted ancient maple at the back of their house, an unfinished house that looks like it will never be finished. The girl is too big for the swing and her butt hardly fits through the hollow opening of the tire. She turns herself around until the rope gets twisted real good, then lets go and it spins her like a top. I'd be too embarrassed to play on a swing at her age. I grow dizzy watching. (2000, 17)

I love the way this passage sounds as if Tamara is recording a scene out her bedroom window as it is happening. I also love how reflective she is. Which lines reveal her opinions about the scene she is viewing?

In Sheri Reynolds' novel *The Rapture of Canaan*, the main character is a young girl named Ninah. Ninah becomes interested in a classmate named Ajita. The author writes,

> She came to school that day wearing the cutest pants I'd ever seen, green ones with tiny pink flowers printed all over them. And they got tight at the ankles, and at the top where the elastic went, they had strings to pull them tight around her waist, and at the bottom of each string was a tiny bell so that when she moved, she tinkled and chimed just a little. She had on a white shirt tucked into those pants, and her hair was pulled back in a French braid, the kind my mamma didn't know how to do, and at the bottom where her velvety black braid touched the middle of her back, she had a ribbon made out of the same fabric as her pants. She had silver rings through her ears, and even though she was smaller than I was, she looked so much older. (1995, 84)

This passage demonstrates what a keen observer Ninah is, but it also demonstrates that she has learned to weave her thinking into her observations. Which lines tell us that Ninah has strong feelings about this girl's appearance?

Have any of you tried to combine observations of things you were interested in with your thoughts and feelings about them?

Books Noted in this Lesson

Some Things That Stay Sarah Willis
The Rapture of Canaan Sheri Reynolds

LESSON 39

Imagining Our Lives in a Book

Many people say that literature is like a window and a mirror. The books we read force us to see the world and to see ourselves in new ways. When we write about ourselves, our families, and the experiences we know best, we also want to think about these topics in new ways. We don't want to sound bland or ordinary. Frances, the main character in Alice Mattison's novel *Hilda and Pearl*, has an unusual way of thinking fresh thoughts about her life. She imagines that she and her family members are characters in a book and wonders how her family experiences would turn out if they were being written about in a book.

For example, at one point in the story she removes a pair of unfamiliar and somewhat mysterious baby shoes from her mother's dresser drawer without her mother's knowledge or permission. The author writes,

> In a book, the girl who had taken the shoes would tell her mother, and in the end, she and her mother would be closer because of it. The mother would draw the girl up against her, on her lap or next to her if the girl was big, and tell her the whole story. Maybe they would cry together . . . (1995, 113)

When Frances' father has problems at work, again the young girl thinks, "If they were people in a book, Frances would have suggested that they pray, but she had never heard anyone in her family pray and wasn't sure how to go about it" (117).

I wonder if Frances' technique could help some of you when you are trying to generate new thoughts in your writer's notebooks? Just as an experiment, you might look back at an old entry and imagine the people and events as being part of a book in the library. You might even begin the way Frances does, with the words "In a book, . . ." See where this thinking leads you. Do you gain new insights? Do any new problems or solutions become obvious? Do you have any different opinions or changes in point of view?

Books Noted in this Lesson

Hilda and Pearl Alice Mattison

LESSON 40

Relying on Metaphors and Similes

Metaphors and similes are of course important tools for writers. I have been reading an adult novel with a most unusual title, *The Curious Incident of the Dog in the Night-Time,* written by Mark Haddon. Christopher, the young boy who is the main character, suggests that metaphors can make people's speech confusing. He lists the following as metaphors:

> I laughed my socks off.
> He was the apple of her eye.
> They had a skeleton in the closet.
> We had a real pig of a day.
> The dog was stone dead. (2004, 15)

Metaphors can be confusing, especially if you've never heard them before and don't understand what they mean. The truth is, even though Christopher finds these metaphors confusing, they are quite common ones and are used by many people. Today, I want to talk about more original ones.

When crafted well, metaphors and similes shouldn't be confusing but should help the reader really understand the author's intent. It's important when you decide to use such literary language that you stay clear of any clichés. For example, I don't want to hear that you have butterflies in your stomach when you are nervous. People say that too often. Besides, I am not really sure having butterflies flittering around in your tummy adequately describes being nervous. Surely there are better ways to capture that feeling. Do any come to mind?

So please remember, your pillow doesn't have to be as soft as a marshmallow, your father is not as tall as a giraffe, and in all likelihood, your baby sister does not roar like a lion.

I was very struck by Addy, the main character in a novel titled *All the Finest Girls*, by Alexandra Styron. The author frequently helps the reader understand the story by choosing very powerful metaphors and similes. For example, Styron gives Addy the following words when she has cut her hand badly and her nanny, Louise, takes her to the doctor:

> Dr. Goodman has hair like cauliflower. He holds a needle up to the light, so big he could use it to make clothes for a giant. The room is chilly and smells like my father's favorite drink. I'm sitting on a table covered in paper that crinkles under my legs, and I'm frightened and my finger throbs. Louise holds my good hand in hers. Together they look like chocolate and butter . . .
>
> The first stitch feels like burning water. Louise holds me tight. Zigzag goes the cloth of her coat. Zigzag. Zigzag. Louise smiles at me. Zigzag. On and on, the burning water on my hand and zigzag. Zigzag.
>
> "That should do it."
>
> Dr. Goodman is finished. I look at the fatty part of my pointing finger. It's rusty brown from the medicine the nurse swabbed on, and across it run four black X's, just like the stitching on the back of my blue jeans. It's swollen and pulses with heat. The nurse has begun to gently roll gauze around my hand when the door springs open. All in a sweet-smelling rush, Mom appears, waved in I think by an unseen magic wand. Her butterscotch hair is falling from its twist . . .
>
> Back at home, Mom rushes about turning on all the lights till the house glows like a birthday cake. (2001, 49)

Which metaphors and similes work for you? Which stand out? Which ones are the most surprising?

In Toni Morrison's book *The Bluest Eye*, young Pecola vomits. Here's how the author describes the incident:

> The puke swaddles down the pillow onto the sheet—green-gray, with flecks of orange. It moves like the inside of an uncooked egg. Stubbornly clinging to its own mass, refusing to break up and be removed. How I wonder, can it be so neat and nasty at the same time? (1970, 13)

Here, Toni Morrison proves that you can even write about such a distasteful thing as vomit in a most poetic way. In addition to the simile comparing the movement of the puke to the inside of an uncooked egg, I also appreciate the strong verb *swaddles* in the first sentence and the thoughtful question that closes the passage.

Elsewhere in the book, Pecola also describes her father's face. Morrison writes,

> My daddy's face is a study. Winter moves into it and presides there. His eyes become a cliff of snow threatening to avalanche; his eyebrows bend like black limbs of leafless trees. His skin takes on the pale, cheerless yellow of winter sun; for a jaw he has the edges of a snowbound field dotted with stubble; his high forehead is the frozen sweep of the Erie, hiding currents of gelid thoughts that eddy in the darkness. Wolf killer turned hawk fighter, he worked night and day to keep one from the door and one from under the windowsills. A Vulcan guarding the flames, he gives us instructions about which doors to keep closed or opened for proper distribution of heat, lays kindling nearby, discusses qualities of coal, and teaches us how to rake, feed and bank the fire. And he will not unrazor his lips until spring. (52)

Pecola's descriptions, filled with metaphor and simile, make it easy to picture this man's face. You could probably draw his face from such a carefully crafted description.

When you write today, why not begin by rereading your work and searching for places in which a metaphor or simile worked for you or a place in which one might effectively serve your readers? I will be interested in hearing the ways in which you've used these techniques when I come around to confer with you today. And we can share these examples with the class at the end of writing time.

Books Noted in this Lesson

The Curious Incident of the Dog in the Night-Time Mark Haddon

All the Finest Girls Alexandra Styron

The Bluest Eye Toni Morrison

LESSON 41

Making Reading-Writing Connections

Children the world over share common experiences. I am never surprised, therefore, when teachers from faraway places tell me that their young students write about topics similar to yours. In any classroom, you can probably find notebook entries or completed writing projects about visits to grandparents' homes, important sports games, best friends, and so on. Of course, each writer has something different to say and a unique way of saying it.

Sometimes when I am reading novels for pleasure, the young characters in the book talk about a topic that I have seen many of you attempt to capture on paper. I have decided to collect passages about popular student topics, creating a scrapbook that you can refer to at any time.

For example, many of you write about animals—taking care of your pets, playing with your stuffed animals, or visiting the zoo. One of the passages I will mount in my scrapbook is from a novel called *The Life of Pi*, by Yann Martel. The young main character has the unique experience of being the son of a zookeeper. The book is filled with rich descriptions of animals. At one point in the story, the author writes:

> On my way out I might stop by the terraria to look at some shiny frogs glazed bright, bright green, or yellow and deep blue, or brown and pale green. Or it might be birds that caught my attention: pink flamingoes or black swans or one-wattled cassowaries, or something smaller, silver diamond doves, Cape glossy starlings, peach-faced lovebirds, Nanday conures, orange-fronted parakeets. Not likely that the elephants, the seals, the big cats or the bears would be up and doing, but the baboons, the macaques, the mangabeys, the gibbons, the deer,

> the tapirs, the llamas, the giraffes, the mongooses were early risers. Every morning before I was out the main gate I had one last impression that was both ordinary and unforgettable: a pyramid of turtles; the iridescent snout of a mandrill; the stately silence of a giraffe; the obese, yellow open mouth of a hippo; the beak-and-claw climbing of a macaw parrot up a wire fence; the greeting claps of a shoebill's bill; the senile lecherous expression of a camel. And all these riches were had quickly, as I hurried to school. It was after school that I discovered in a leisurely way what it's like to have an elephant search your clothes in the friendly hope of finding a hidden nut, or an orang-utan pick through your hair for tick snacks, its wheeze of disappointment at what an empty pantry your head is. I wish I could convey the perfection of a seal slipping into water or a spider monkey swinging from point to point or a lion merely turning its head. But language founders in such seas. Better to picture it in your head if you want to feel it. (2001, 14–15)

Of course, none of us would have such exotic adventures in a zoo, but we can take lessons in how to write well about animals from the way this author has crafted his words. Notice, for instance, that he doesn't just say *birds.* He mentions their precise names—*pink flamingoes, black swans, silver diamond doves.* Notice he doesn't just say *monkeys.* Instead, he writes *baboons, macaques, gibbons.*

Notice too how he focuses in on distinctive features of the animals—the lecherous expression of the camel, the clap of the shoebill's bill, the yellow open mouth of the hippo. Then, too, he shows the animals in action—the seal slipping into water, the spider monkey swinging from point to point.

The author also fills the passage with long list sentences, which makes us feel that he is really an authority on life in a zoo, making us sense the lushness of the setting.

How many of these techniques could you borrow when you are writing about your pets at home?

(See the following excerpts about other popular kid topics:

Being home alone, on page 70 in Donna Tartt's book *The Little Friend* [2002]
Moving to a new home, on pages 48–49 and 134 in Elizabeth Berg's *Durable Goods* [1993]
Reading your writing aloud to your class, on page 374 of Jodi Picoult's *My Sister's Keeper* [2004] and pages 41–45 in Jamaica Kincaid's *Annie John* [1983]

Love of a skateboard, on pages 244–45 in Jodi Picoult's *My Sister's Keeper* [2004]

Snowfall, on page 309 of Ann-Marie MacDonald's novel *The Way the Crow Flies* [2003], on pages 86–87 in Rebecca Wells' *Ya-Yas in Bloom* [2005], and on page 5 in Pete Hamill's *Snow in August* [1997]

See also a description of snowfall from a child's point of view on page 48 in Khaled Hosseini's novel *The Kite Runner* [2003] [on page 4 in this book] and page 170 in Kate Atkinson's *Behind the Scenes at the Museum* [on page 73 in this book].

It might be helpful to enlarge all five snow passages and place them side by side, encouraging students to talk about their effectiveness and the various literary techniques used by these very different writers.)

Books Noted in this Lesson

The Life of Pi Yann Martel

The Little Friend Donna Tartt

Durable Goods Elizabeth Berg

My Sister's Keeper Jodi Picoult

The Way the Crow Flies Ann-Marie MacDonald

Ya-Yas in Bloom Rebecca Wells

Snow in August Pete Hamill

Annie John Jamaica Kincaid

The Kite Runner Khaled Hosseini

Behind the Scenes at the Museum Kate Atkinson

LESSON 42

Presenting Ordinary Life

Not only do beginning writers often make the mistake of thinking that only extraordinary or special events in their lives are worth writing about, but they also think that the way to impress their readers is to add a lot of fancy adjectives.

In Seamus Deane's novel *Reading in the Dark* (1996), the unnamed narrator, a young boy, becomes embarrassed about his own writing at school when his teacher shares a well-written essay created by one of his peers. The author writes:

> The English teacher read aloud a model essay which had been, to our surprise, written by a country boy. It was an account of his mother setting the table for the evening meal and then waiting until his father came in from the fields ... Everything was so simple, especially the way they waited ...

The young boy comments,

> I'd never thought such stuff was worth writing about. It was ordinary life- ...

And then the young boy goes on to admit

> I felt embarrassed because my own essay had been full of long and strange words I had found in the dictionary—"cerulean," "azure," "phantasm," and "implacable"...

Not only did the young boy fill his essay with show-off words, but he also used them to describe the kind of sky and ocean he had only read about in novels, never witnessed himself.

The lessons that the narrator learned are important for all of us to remember. First, pick topics that you really know and care about. And second, to really write well about them, do not try to impress your reader with flowery language. Instead, rely on specific and accurate information. As the teacher in the novel suggests after sharing the model essay,

> "Now that," said the master, "that's writing. That's just telling the truth." (See complete passages on pages 20–21.)

Those of you who are working toward publication might consider heeding the advice offered in this novel. Reread your work and make sure you haven't filled your pages with flowery language. Instead, give your readers the essential and honest information they need to understand your meaning.

Books Noted in this Lesson

Reading in the Dark Seamus Deane

PART FOUR

On Loving Language

LESSON 43

Caring About and Learning New Words

Writers are curious about words and always eager to learn new words and expressions. Whether they are reading, eavesdropping on conversations, or talking to family and friends, they discover many ways to hold onto these words and to figure out their meanings.

Over the weekend I was reading a novel titled *Snow in August*, by Pete Hamill. As I read it, I kept thinking that the main character, a young boy named Michael, would be a great student to have in our writing class. He is very curious about the world, he becomes passionate about his interests, he loves to learn new languages, he loves to read and to hear his mom tell Irish folktales from her childhood, and he especially cares about words. At one point in the story, on New Year's Eve, he wonders about the song "Auld Lang Syne." I bet many of you have heard that song.

The author writes,

> He wondered what the words meant. *Auld* that's easy, old. But what did *lang* mean? Or *syne*? He couldn't find them in the dictionary and he hoped he would remember to ask his mother about them in the morning. (1997, 61)

Have any of you ever wondered about what those words must mean, or looked up their meanings in a dictionary, or asked a grown-up for their definitions? Can you share any other occasions in which you went out of your way to learn the meaning of unfamiliar words?

At one point in Faith Sullivan's book *The Cape Ann*, six-year-old Lark's mom used an expression that the child didn't understand. She referred to something as a "cheap trick." The author writes:

> "What does that mean?" I'd asked.
>
> "Never mind. It doesn't matter. Forget I said that."
>
> But I didn't forget. I memorized her words. When someone said something that I didn't understand, something that I wanted to remember until I was old enough to understand, I memorized the words or I *used* to memorize the words. Now I printed them in the back of my first confession notebook. Once in awhile I read them just to see if I understood yet. (1988, 67)

Each of you can do likewise, reserving a place in your writer's notebook for words and expressions that you find interesting, but also puzzling.

In Edwidge Danticat's novel *Breath, Eyes, Memory*, the young child Sophie visits her grandmother with her aunt Tante Atie. She hears her grandmother talk of "an attack of chagrin" and ponders that phrase. Danticat writes,

> We left the next day to return to Croix-des-Rosets. Tante Atie had to go back to work. Besides, my grandmother said that it was best that we leave before she got too used to us and suffered an attack of chagrin.
>
> To my grandmother, chagrin was a genuine physical disease. Like a hurt leg or a broken arm. To treat chagrin, you drank tea leaves that only my grandmother and other wise old women could recognize.
>
> We each gave my grandmother two kisses as she urged us to go before she kept us for good.
>
> "Can you really die of chagrin?" I asked Tante Atie in the van on the way back . . . (1994, 24–25)

This little girl didn't write expressions down in the back of her notebook. Instead, when she was curious about the meaning of words and phrases, she asked the adults around her. Good for her. If you were to do likewise, you would find it much easier to find just the right words when you write.

In another novel that I have been reading, called *Shadow Baby*, by Alison McGhee, an eleven-year-old girl named Clara is also interested in words. In fact, her teacher labels her a "word-person," and throughout the novel, Clara comments about her favorite words. At one point, she says,

> Tragic is a good word. It would be a good name too, with the soft middle "g," except it's not a name. You couldn't name a baby Tragic. That would be a travesty, which is also a beautiful-sounding word. Travis is the closest you could come to that one. (2000, 18)

In addition to their meanings, this child pays particular attention to the sounds of words and their spellings. She loves words so much that she considers some words to be in her "personal category of perfection." What words would you choose if you were to create such a list of perfect words? What would your choices be based upon?

(For more of Clara's comments about words, see pages 7, 22, 61, 137, and 176 in *Shadow Baby*. See also the descriptions of Vocabulary Day, a family dinner tradition, on pages 60 and 82 in Elizabeth Berg's *What We Keep* [1998].)

Books Noted in this Lesson

Snow in August Pete Hamill

The Cape Ann Faith Sullivan

Breath, Eyes, Memory Edwidge Danticat

Shadow Baby Alison McGhee

What We Keep Elizabeth Berg

LESSON 44

Using Precise Language

Even though we sometimes go to a thesaurus, searching for an alternative word to use instead of the one that first came to mind, the truth is, each word listed in a thesaurus entry, although similar in meaning, is different from the others.

It's obvious that the words *sound* different. How they work in combination with other words in your sentence will also be different. And their meanings, even if close, are also slightly different. You have to be fussy about choosing the right one, the one that has the most precise meaning. Of course, the word also has to sound right in your sentence.

There's a passage in Pete Hamill's *Snow in August* that speaks to the importance of using precise language. The main character, a young boy named Michael, begins to wonder about the word *horse.* Hamill writes:

> The letters H-O-R-S-E were combined into *horse.* But what kind of horse? Which horse? ... There were big police horses and small horses people rode in Prospect Park in the summertime and the racehorses that men in Casement's bar bet on with Brendan the bookmaker. There were colts and stallions and ponies and yearlings, pintos and broncos, steeds and mustangs and those were just the horses he'd learned about at the movies in the Venus. And down at the lumberyard at the bottom of Collins Street they used sawhorses, which were made of wood! (1997, 84).

Michael is right: there are so many words that refer to different kinds of horses. And if he were writing about a particular horse, it would be important for him to choose the most precise one, the one that would tell the reader exactly what he meant.

In another book I have read, called *The House on Mango Street*, by Sandra Cisneros, a young girl named Esperanza has the following conversation with her friends:

> The Eskimos got thirty different names for snow, I say. I read it in a book.
>
> I got a cousin, Rachel says. She got three different names.
>
> There ain't thirty different kinds of snow, Lucy says.
>
> There are two kinds. The clean kind and the dirty kind, clean and dirty. Only two.
>
> There are a million zillion kinds, says Nenny. No two exactly alike. Only how do you remember which one is which?
>
> She got three last names and, let me see, two first names. One in English and one in Spanish . . .
>
> And clouds got at least ten different names, I say.
>
> Names for clouds? Nenny asks. Names just like you and me?
>
> That up there, that's cumulus, and everybody looks up . . . (1984, 35–36)

When you are writing today, I want you to pay particular attention to the words you use, making sure you are fussy about choosing just the right one. Don't say you have a dog; tell us you have a cocker spaniel or a French poodle or a Chihuahua. Don't tell us you live in a house. Tell us if it is an apartment, a ranch, a brownstone. And of course, if a description of the sky is important in your writing, you might mention the exact name of the clouds.

Books Noted in this Lesson

Snow in August Pete Hamill

The House on Mango Street Sandra Cisneros

LESSON 45

Playing with Language

Words are so important to writers, and playing with words is one way of appreciating their sounds and meanings and becoming fussy about their arrangements when you write.

In a novel titled *Peace Like a River*, written by Leif Enger, the young main character, Reuben, plays with words with his sister Swede. Their father is about to stop for gas at a place called Dale's Oil Company. Although the sign out front reads "Closed," the dad remarks,

> "I believe we might prevail on Dale. What do you think?"
>
> "Prevail on Dale," I repeated to Swede.
>
> "To make a sale," she added.
>
> "And if we fail, we'll whale on Dale—"
>
> "Till he needs Braille!"
>
> "Will you guys desist?" Dad asked. (2001, 176)

That's one way to play with language.

At another point in the story, Reuben is asked to comment on the quality of a pork dish he is served, made with meat that came from a pig named Emil. His father's friend, Waltzer, asks him to be really honest about the taste. The author writes,

> "Take a bite, Reuben. Describe the flavor."
>
> I bit. The pork had been boiled a long time. Indeed it bore no trace of salt. It was like chewing a hank of old rope. Waltzer's eyes were alight and curious. Desperately I sought the elusive civil adjective.

"It's pretty good," I told him.

"I commend your courtesy; but nonsense. I won't take offense. Nor will Emil. Do it for Emil, hm?"

You remember Emil.

I peered at the pork. Waltzer said, "Go on. Assess the piquancy of Emil. It's all the memorial he's bound to get. Poor little Emil." He was delighted the meat had a name, he couldn't use it enough.

And yet, surprisingly, knowing the pale lump before me was Emil was not disturbing. In fact it freed me up somehow. I chewed him and swallowed him. "It's—stiff," I said cautiously. "A little dry."

Waltzer said, "Go on."

"It's dull. Blunt."

"Yes, yes." Waltzer liked this. A strange thing occurred: adjectives, generally standoffish around me, began tossing themselves at my feet. "It's fibrous. Rough. Ropy." I was faintly aware of insulting Sara's cookery, but Waltzer was nodding, smiling. His favor was better than the alternative. I basked in it: and it was fun, for a change, having the words. "Dispirited, stagnant. Mortified. Vapid." I wasn't sure what the last one meant, having heard it from Swede in a discussion about her second-grade teacher, but it had a ring.

"Well said," Waltzer declared . . . (266–67)

What an incredible passage. I am not quite sure why adjectives began tossing themselves at Reuben's feet, but it certainly sounded like he was having fun. Imagine knowing so many adjectives that you could make a long list to describe something that you care for or something you dislike.

Just as an exercise today, you might think of something that you are interested in describing or evaluating and try to make a long list of carefully chosen and very specific adjectives. Knowing such words might come in handy one day.

Books Noted in this Lesson

Peace Like a River Leif Enger

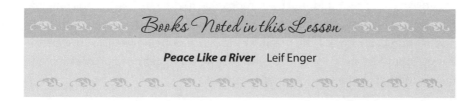

LESSON 46

Browsing the Dictionary

Since writers love words so much, it follows that they are also interested in parts of words and the letters of the alphabet that make up those words. There is a young student in a novel I am reading who competes in spelling bees, and her family is helping her prepare for a big competition. Her name is Eliza and she is a main character in *Bee Season*, by Myla Goldberg. At one point in the story the author describes Eliza's fascination with the alphabet. Listen to this passage:

> Paging through the dictionary is like looking through a microscope. Every word breaks down into parts with unique properties—prefix, suffix, roots. Eliza gleans not only the natural laws that govern the letters but their individual behaviors. R, M and D are strong, unbending and faithful. The sometimes silent B and G and the slippery K follow strident codes of conduct. Even the redoubtable H, which can make P sound like F and turn ROOM into Rheum, obeys etymology. Consonants are the camels of language, proudly carrying their lingual loads.
>
> Vowels, however, are a different species, the fish that flash and glisten in the watery depths. Vowels are elastic and inconstant, fickle and unfaithful. E can sound like I or U. -IBLE and -ABLE are impossible to discern. There is no combination the vowels haven't tried, exhausted and incestuous in their couplings. E will just as soon pair with A, J, or O, leading the dance or being led. Eliza prefers the vowels' unpredictability and, of all vowels, favors Y. Y defies categorization, the only letter that can be two things at once. (2002, 49)

I so appreciate the thought that "Paging through the dictionary is like looking through a microscope." Perhaps we need to carve out time to browse all the dictionaries in our classroom, adding others from the school library and some from our homes. We can then record and share our own surprising discoveries.

Are there spellings that surprise you? Meanings that intrigue you? Interesting etymologies to share?

What do you think of Eliza's comments about the letters of the alphabet? Do you see letters as having distinct personalities?

Eliza studies the dictionary to prepare for a spelling bee. What are other ways to improve our skill as spellers? Why is it important to do so?

Books Noted in this Lesson

Bee Season Myla Goldberg

PART FIVE

On Learning from Fictional Readers and Writers

LESSON 47

Making a Place for Reading

I think the best place in this school to learn to be a great writer is the library. Writers take their reading very seriously. When they read, they discover topics for their own writing. They become interested in new genres and formats. They study authors' techniques to learn how to improve their own writing. They develop mentor relationships with their favorite writers, aspiring to be more like them.

I am always thrilled when the children in the novels I read are devoted readers. It makes me want Madeleine, Rachel, Eliza, Siddalee, Clara, and Amir to be real so they could visit the classroom and tell you why reading has become so important in their lives.

In Ann-Marie MacDonald's book *The Way the Crow Flies*, the main character, Madeleine, is a devoted reader. The author writes,

> Afterwards, in bed with a book, the spell of television feels remote compared to the journey into the page. To be in a book. To slip into the crease where two pages meet, to live in the place where your eyes alight upon the words to ignite a world of smoke and peril, colour and serene delight. That is a journey no one can end with the change of a channel. Enduring magic. She opens *Peter Pan*. (2003, 123)

It comes as no surprise that in this novel, Madeleine grows up to be a writer. People who love books so much often crave to create their own. I wonder if anyone in this room can honestly say that he or she prefers reading over watching television?

In Pearl Abraham's novel *The Romance Reader*, the main character, a girl named Rachel, longs to have her own collection of books. Here's how she pictures that collection:

> One day, I will have my own bookcase. On my shelves I'll have at least one book for every letter of the alphabet, with room for more. They'll be my books. I'll build a bookcase like Father built; it takes up a whole wall in our new dining room. I helped with the trim. I hammered small finishing nails into the wood scalloping on the edge of each shelf and into the carved strip of wood on the sides. In my bookcase, every book will have its place, like Father's books, and if I take one out, I'll put it back where it came from. (1995, 39)

Many of you are lucky enough to have your own bookcase at home. If you didn't own a bookcase or any books of your own, would you feel as strongly as Rachel does?

Eliza, the champion speller in Myla Goldberg's novel *Bee Season*, reveals how deeply books touch her, especially William Steig's *Sylvester and the Magic Pebble.* Eliza hasn't been feeling very good about herself lately; she's been feeling not very special and sort of left out. The author writes,

> Eliza can sense herself changing. She has often felt that her outsides were too dull for her insides, that deep within her there was something better than what everyone else could see. Perhaps, like the donkey in her favorite bedtime story, she had been turned into stone. Perhaps, if she could only find a magic pebble, she could change. Walking home from school, Eliza has often looked for a pebble, red and round, that might transform her from her unremarkable self. When Eliza finds this pebble in her dreams, her name becomes the first the teacher memorizes at the beginning of the school year . . . (2002, 45)

Has any book ever touched you so deeply that it made its way into your dreams?

In Rebecca Wells' novel *Little Altars Everywhere*, Siddalee's mother talks about her daughter's love of reading. She says,

> Sidda can't help herself. She just loves books. Loves the way they feel, the way they smell, loves those black letters marching across the white pages. When Sidda falls in love with a book, she is positive that she is the first person in the

> world to have discovered it, poor child. Thinks that no one else anywhere, anytime, has ever heard of the book.
>
> I'll never forget the time she flipped over *The Secret Garden*, which Buggy gave her. She lived inside that book for days. You couldn't even talk to the child. Then, after a while, she went to the library and looked that book up, and when she found out that other copies existed and all kinds of people had their names on the borrower's card, she just broke down in tears. She had truly believed that she was the only one who had ever read that book! After that, everywhere she went she stared at people, trying to figure out which one of them had trespassed on her book. (1992, 51)

Have you ever loved a book so much that you didn't want to share it with anyone else? Have you ever felt that a book was meant for your eyes only? Why do you think you had such a strong attachment to that particular book?

(See also Clara's lament about books being thrown in the trash on page 60 of Alison McGhee's *Shadow Baby* [2000] and the passage about Amir spending his allowance on books on page 19 of Khaled Hosseini's *The Kite Runner* [2003].)

Books Noted in this Lesson

The Way the Crow Flies Ann-Marie MacDonald

The Romance Reader Pearl Abraham

Bee Season Myla Goldberg

Little Altars Everywhere Rebecca Wells

Shadow Baby Alison McGhee

The Kite Runner Khaled Hosseini

LESSON 48

Rereading Favorite Texts

When writers find books that they admire, they often read them over and over again. Sometimes they read them so often that they commit parts to memory. Has that ever happened to any of you?

I think that knowing books by heart is a very good thing for a writer to do. When you write you can almost feel the rhythm of those well-crafted words inside you. Your own writing may improve because you can't help being influenced by the sound of the words that are inside you.

In Liz Jensen's book *The Ninth Life of Louis Drax*, a doctor comments on the main character, a young French boy named Louis. The author writes,

> Little boys love sea monsters. If I had a son, I'd take him to see the giant squid that's just arrived in Paris, fifteen meters long and pickled in formaldehyde. I saw a photo in *Nouvel Observateur*: a tubular body with suckered tentacles trailing balletically behind. It made me think of an orchid, or a slender grasping sea anemone loosed from its moorings and wandering fathoms deep, lost and racked by doubt. The Latin name is *architeuthis*. In years gone by they were dismissed as a sailors' myth, the product of too much time spent on too much ocean, salt-water madness. But now, global warming has blessed the giant squid; its population has gone berserk, and proof of its existence is daily flotsam on foreign shores. Its eyes are the size of dinner plates.
>
> If I had a son—
>
> But I don't . . . A boy has all the time in the world for a giant squid.

> Louis Drax would have loved to see one, I'm sure of it. He kept pet hamsters, but he hankered after more threatening creatures: tarantulas, iguanas, snakes, bats—gothic animals with spikes, scales, scary fur, a potential for destruction. His favourite reading was a lavishly illustrated children's book called *Les Animaux: leur vie extraordinaire.* He knew much of the text by heart. (2004, 14)

I think Louis would be a great participant in our writing workshop for several reasons. First, he is drawn to a topic, animals, preferably rather dangerous ones. Second, he has a favorite book. And third, he knows much of the text by heart.

(See also Harriet rereading favorite passages from Rudyard Kipling's *The Jungle Book* on page 157 in Donna Tartt's *The Little Friend* [2002]. Also read Amir's description of a very special school activity on page 19 in Khaled Hosseini's *The Kite Runner* [2003]. The children played a game in which they had to recite poetry. After the first student spoke, the next student had one minute to think of a poem to recite that began with the same letter that ended the first poem.

And look at Pi's desire to have a book to read over and over again on pages 207–8 in Yann Martel's *The Life of Pi* [2001].)

Books Noted in this Lesson

The Ninth Life of Louis Drax Liz Jensen

The Little Friend Donna Tartt

The Kite Runner Khaled Hosseini

The Life of Pi Yann Martel

LESSON 49

Becoming Well-Read in One Genre

In Dorothy Allison's *Cavedweller*, the main character, young Cissy, is a devoted reader of science fiction. When she meets up with a young boy named Nolan, she is delighted that they share the same reading preferences. No doubt, if these youngsters were real, I would urge them to try their hand at science fiction writing. The author writes:

> Cissy never forgot the first few times she saw Nolan, planted on his mama's porch every afternoon with a different paperback book in his hand. It was the books that drew her . . . she walked up to the porch and asked Nolan what he was reading, but Nolan just pushed his glasses up his sweaty nose and held out the book, a pristine copy of *Starship Troopers* by Robert Heinlein.
>
> "You read *Stranger*?" Cissy asked.
>
> "I've read 'em all. Only one I don't reread is *Podkayne.* That one got on my nerves." . . .
>
> "You like science fiction then?" Nolan asked.
>
> "Yeah."
>
> Nolan put *Starship Troopers* down with a scrap of ribbon marking his place. "Come on," he said, and led her around to the back of the house and down into the basement. Along one wall of the workshop his daddy rarely used there were four tall bookshelves built just to hold paperbacks. Each was crammed tightly, books sorted alphabetically by author and marked with little cardboard dividers.
>
> "My collection." Nolan's voice was deep with pride. (1998, 126–27)

Cissy and Nolan certainly know the world of science fiction writers. It's very important that each of you have favorite writers in each of the genres that you are writing in. If I asked, "Who are your favorite nonfiction writers?" "Who are the poets you admire?" or "Who are the picture book writers you'd like to take lessons from?" I expect that each of you would have an answer.

It would also be helpful in this classroom if we knew who the expert readers are in each genre. That way we would know whom to go to for information and recommendations. Just as there are designated drivers, we can announce designated readers. I am going to post all the genres we read and then leave room for you to add your name if that kind of reading is your specialty. I will be posting poetry, memoir, biography, realistic fiction, editorials, letters to the editor, book reviews, picture books, feature articles, how-to texts, and others.

It would also be interesting to know if anyone in the class has begun collecting books. We can also post information about your collections so that we can count on you as a resource as well as share information about additional titles for your collections. Perhaps we can even begin swapping books to add to one another's growing collections.

Books Noted in this Lesson

Cavedweller Dorothy Allison

LESSON 50

Taking Notes on Reading

Some people always have paper and pens on their night tables just in case an important thought comes to them late at night when they are trying to fall asleep or even in the middle of the night if they awake and have trouble falling back to sleep. Then, too, bedtime reading can inspire important ideas that people want to record. Perhaps we should all keep our writer's notebook next to our bed at night, just in case we need to do some nighttime jottings.

In *Snow in August* by Pete Hamill, young Michael's bedtime reading gives him ideas about his own life, making him think about his friends. If he were a writer, his reading would certainly inspire ideas for his writing. One night, he falls asleep reading *The Three Musketeers.* The author writes:

> The title of the book wasn't really accurate because there were actually four musketeers, but in the end, that didn't matter. What mattered was their slogan, their motto: All for one, and one for all. That's the way he and Sonny and Jimmy were. Even when they disagreed on some things, they were together. Friends. Musketeers. He was thinking about that when he fell asleep. (1997, 61)

If we read powerful books, the ideas should make us think about our own lives and the lives of others. The ideas in the book should force us to reflect on the world around us. These reflections belong in our writer's notebooks.

In Chris Bohjalian's *The Buffalo Soldier,* the main character, a young boy named Alfred, becomes very interested in a book given to him by a neighbor. The book tells the story of the black cavalry men of the old West, and Alfred can't stop thinking about these heroic soldiers. One night, when he has trouble sleeping, he shuts his eyes . . . Listen to this passage:

> For a brief moment he imagined he was buffalo soldier George Rowe, half-asleep somewhere in Texas, confident even though it was night and his detachment was far from its fort. Rowe was disciplined and sharp; he didn't care that he was an outsider. He'd won a medal. He was Alfred's favorite of the black men he'd met in the book.
>
> In his mind he traced the outlines of the boulders and scrub pine that might have surrounded Rowe's camp, and then slowly watched those shapes transformed into the more familiar contours of the furniture in his room and the objects that sat upon them. He burrowed into the closet, envisioning exactly what was there on the floor. His backpack. The photo album. Food. (2002, 173–74)

I wonder if any of you have been so moved by a book that you thought about it when you were getting ready to fall asleep. I wonder if any of you have ever been so touched by a book that you became one of the characters in your daydreams or night dreams, when you were awake or asleep. How do you think a book that moves you so deeply might influence your writing?

In *The Kite Runner* by Khaled Hosseini (2003), the main character, Amir, when just a youngster, becomes curious about his friend Hassan, a member of the Hazaras sect of Afghanistan (see page 9). He wants to know why Hassan and his people are treated differently than the members of Amir's own family. He sneaks an old history book from his father's study into his bedroom late at night and stays up reading about the Hazara history.

Have you ever been so curious about something that you were willing to sneak books into your bed late at night, even reading by flashlight after your parents thought you were asleep? Did you sneak those books because your family members don't want you to read that genre or that topic, or did you have to sneak the reading in because you were supposed to be asleep?

Books Noted in this Lesson

Snow in August Pete Hamill
The Buffalo Soldier Chris Bohjalian
The Kite Runner Khaled Hosseini

LESSON 51

Reading for Information

Writers, like all of us, read for many reasons. They read to be reminded of things in their own lives and to be inspired to think about people with different lives. They read and reread favorite authors to learn from them and study their literary craft. They read to immerse themselves in favorite genres. They also refer to books when they need to research information for their own works.

Michael, the main character in Pete Hamill's *Snow in August*, turns to books to satisfy his curiosity about the world. He becomes curious when he learns that Jewish people live in his neighborhood. He decides to learn about them by looking them up in his encyclopedia. He learns many surprising things about Jewish people and realizes that he now has many more questions. He even has the urge to wake his mother in the middle of the night to ask her his questions. The author writes,

> If there were two million Jews in New York City, where did they live? Where were their kids? Did they play stickball? Were they Dodger fans? Did they pitch pennies in the summer and trade comic books and read about Captain Marvel? Why weren't more of them around *here*?
>
> He wanted to wake his mother and ask her all these questions. He wanted to tell her about his discoveries, about the Jewish laws and the health codes and the alphabet. He wanted to ask her why all those Jews had been killed by Hitler if *even before the war* everybody knew what he was up to. He wanted to ask her if she'd ever heard Jewish music and where the two million Jews lived in the city of New York. (1997, 51)

Michael's reading pushed him to ask more questions, and if he had had a writer's notebook, he would have had the perfect place to record his questions, his tentative answers to those questions, and, as time went on, the factual answers to his questions. This is an important way all of us can use our writer's notebooks. We can read about things that interest us, record our questions, reflect on those questions, and then record any answers we discover as we talk to people, read additional material, make firsthand observations, search the Internet, and so on.

Books Noted in this Lesson

Snow in August Pete Hamill

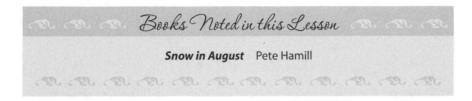

LESSON 52

Thinking About Book Reviews

Just as many of you have become better writers by talking to one another about the way you get ideas, the way you borrow techniques from published authors you admire, or the ways you've learned to make your writing more effective, so too, we can also learn from fictional young folks, ones who are presented as taking their writing seriously.

Eleven-year-old Clara, the main character in *Shadow Baby*, a book by Alison McGhee, is a child who loves to read and write. She even makes up her own book reports, reports about nonexistent books, because she can't imagine doing what she considers a trivial assignment about a book she loves. She can't write a book report about a book she likes because she "can't stand what a book report does, boils a book down to a few sentences about plot"(2000, 62). The author continues,

> It hurts me to see a book report. It's painful to me. Book reports are to books what (a) brown sugar and water boiled together until thick are to true maple syrup from Adirondack sugar maples, (b) lukewarm reconstituted nonfat powdered milk is to whipped cream, and (c) a drawing of a roller coaster is to a roller-coaster ride. Give me a *real* assignment, I say. (13)

Clara's comments should make us think about how to write wisely about the books we read. Why are those analogies so effective in helping us understand Clara's attitude toward book reports? What do you think would qualify as a real assignment to Clara?

Perhaps we need to carve out time to begin a course of study about writing worthy and purposeful book reviews. First, we need to make sure that we have real reasons for writing about the books we read. Perhaps our writing will be compiled into a suggested summer reading list for students throughout the grade or printed in the school newsletter as recommendations for holiday gifts. Can you think of any other uses for our written reviews of books?

Then, instead of the traditional school book report, perhaps we should read published book reviews and figure out how professional writers write wisely about books. We can select our favorite book reviewers from the student magazines we read and focus in on their content, style, and literary techniques.

Books Noted in this Lesson

Shadow Baby Alison McGhee

LESSON 53

Thinking About Writing Fiction

Most of you use your writer's notebooks to gather bits and pieces from your lives, beginning thoughts that might lead you to finished, publishable works someday. You jot lists, copy favorite passages, ask questions, respond to your reading, do quick freewrites, attempt to capture people or places, share wonderings, play with language, draft poems, and so on. Occasionally some students use their notebooks to write fiction, a genre that deserves careful study.

In *The Secret Life of Bees*, a novel by Sue Monk Kidd, the main character, Lily, is given a notebook by her friend Zach, after she admits to wanting to be a writer when she grows up. Lily uses the notebook to write fictional stories, but each of them is based on people she knows well and contain some grains of truth connected to these people. Rosaleen had some police troubles. August is a beekeeper. And Zach dreams of becoming a lawyer.

Kidd writes:

> For days I carried the notebook everywhere. I wrote constantly. A made-up story about Rosaleen losing eighty-five pounds, looking so sleek nobody could pick her out of a police lineup. One about August driving a honeymobile around, similar to the bookmobile, only she had jars of honey to dispense instead of books. My favorite though, was one about Zach becoming the . . . lawyer and getting his own television show like Perry Mason. I read it to him during lunch one day, and he listened better than a child at story hour. (2002, 135)

(The author describes Zach as becoming an "ass-busting lawyer." I have omitted the expression for use with our youngest writers.)

Lily is able to capture her readers' attention because she is able to write with authority. She knows these people and their situations well so she can weave in honest, accurate, and believable information. It is also worth noting that Lily pays tribute to the people she loves by making good things happen to them in her stories. She could have chosen the opposite as well—writing stories without happy endings based on people who cause her pain.

When we begin to write fiction, think about whether there are people in your life that you can imagine basing your fictional characters on. Would the lives of these people inspire your storyline as well?

Books Noted in this Lesson

The Secret Life of Bees Sue Monk Kidd

LESSON 54

Feeling Too Close to a Topic

Sometimes writers choose topics that they really care about and yet they still have difficulty writing about them. For example, if your pet recently died, you might choose to write about that sad event because it is on your mind. But when you sit down to write, you might discover that you are not ready to do that writing. The experience is still too raw. Your strong feelings prevent you from putting words on paper.

It can also happen that the topic you choose, one you are really invested in, cannot be written about just yet because you don't have the full picture. For example, say you have been nagging your parents to let you take gymnastics lessons and they have finally agreed and the first one is coming up on Saturday. You decide to write about it today, but then you realize you need to wait until you have actually attended a few classes.

In Linda Ferri's novel *Enchantments* (2005), the main character realizes that she can't write much about her sister, but can write a lot about her brothers, for yet another reason. The author writes,

> For the composition "My Sister" that the teacher assigned me over the Easter holidays, I managed to write only a few lines: that Clara calls anything she really likes "fantasmagoric" and that since she was a little girl she's been attracted by the moon and by astronauts and that when she's happy she starts bouncing on her bed yelling over and over, "Fantasmagoric! Yuri, Gagarin, Yuri!" I can't write more than that, even if I know everything about her, since we're one single being.

With my brothers it's exactly the other way around. I don't know them, but because of the distance between us, I can describe them very well. I see them as members of a small tribe of savages occupying a territory that borders ours but is quite distinct. I witness their daily rituals, I see them kneeling on chairs for hours, absorbed in newspapers spread out on the dinner table; . . . (See complete passage on page 61.)

This young author can't write much about her sister because she is so close to her; she can't seem to separate herself from her subject. She can write about her brothers because she is able to step back, observe, and reflect on them. What do you think of the way she described her brothers?

Can you imagine having a topic that you couldn't write about because it was simply too close to you and you couldn't look at it objectively?

What advice would you give this writer, who is struggling with an assigned topic? What advice would you give the teacher who made the assignment?

Books Noted in this Lesson

Enchantments Linda Ferri

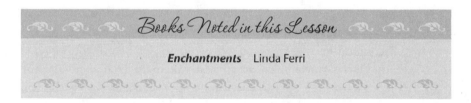

LESSON 55

Composing in Your Mind

I wonder if any of you think about your writing when you are not in school? Have you ever done any composing while you were away from your desk, away from your pencil and paper?

I know that some of my freshest thoughts come to me when my mind is totally at ease—while I am resting in bed, or relaxing in the bath, or daydreaming when I ride the bus. When your mind isn't cluttered, you can receive some really good ideas for your writing. Of course, the challenge is to write them down before you forget them.

In Elizabeth Flock's novel *Me and Emma*, the main character, a young girl named Carrie, has a hard time paying attention to her teacher because she wants to record a letter to her grandmother that she composed in her mind the night before. The author writes,

> I gotta write Gammy while the letter I wrote in my head last night is still fresh.
>
> Dear Gammy,
>
> How are you? I am fine. Emma's fine, too, in case you were wondering. We're hoping you can come on out for a visit and soon. Momma really misses you and we do, too. I have a friend named Orla Mae, isn't that a funny-sounding name? She's real nice, though. You'll like her a lot. There's a dog down a ways named Brownie, only she's black and has three legs.
>
> Please come to see us. We need you.
>
> Love,
> Your granddaughter, Caroline Parker
> P.S. Maybe Auntie Lillibit wants to come on out, too.

> I write all nice with the cursive letters I learned last year in school back home. When Miss Ueland turns to erase the board again I fold it up square by square until it's real tiny and I can squeeze it into my pocket, where it'll stay the rest of the day till I can mail it in town. (2004, 223–24)

If Carrie attended a school that provided regular time to write, she could have written that letter to her grandmother during her workshop time. It's too bad she felt that she had to sneak her writing in behind the teacher's back.

I think Carrie is a fine writer. I especially like the couple of surprising tidbits of information she includes in her letter to her grandmother. What stood out for you? It's also wonderful that she is planning to really mail the letter. Letters are not a school exercise or mere decoration for our bulletin boards. Letters are written to be mailed to real people, and the writer should expect a response.

Carrie composed the letter in her head the night before she wrote it. Have you ever done likewise, planning your writing in your head before you sat down to write?

Books Noted in this Lesson

Me and Emma Elizabeth Flock

LESSON 56

Being Passionate About Poetry

Browsing the novels in my library at home, I found several young main characters who are passionate about writing poetry. As many of you are trying your hand at crafting poems, I thought it would help if I shared some of the things I am learning from these fictional friends.

Leif Enger, in his novel *Peace Like a River*, weaves young Swede's poetry throughout the text. Her brother Reuben, the narrator of the novel, wonders what Swede's teacher must think when his young sister hands in a poem titled, "Sunny Sundown Delivers the Payroll." This rhyming, heroic narrative verse begins with the words

> The men who worked the Redtail Mine were fed up with the boss.
> They swarmed around his office door like blackflies around a hoss. (2001, 26)

(See complete poem on pages 26–27, 34–35, 99–100, 105–6, 160–61, and 258.)

When readers discover that Swede is fascinated with all that is Western, they will not be very surprised that Swede is able to create a lengthy Western adventure about a payroll stagecoach robbery. In commenting on her reading of Western paperbacks, Reuben suggests that his sister "popped them down like Raisinets." Of course, the reader will be impressed with the quality of the writing for such a young writer.

Swede's poetry writing reminds us that poets can write poems about any topic, not just the "usual" topics such as spring, flowers, rainbows, and the moon. Swede's poetry focuses on a topic that she cares and knows about, the West.

Swede also reminds us that poems can tell stories and that we can collect and study narrative poetry. Swede rhymes her poems, but of course, not all poems rhyme. Her poems are filled with very strong meter, an element to be studied by serious poets.

At one point in the story, Swede reads aloud poems by Robert Louis Stevenson to Reuben (page 87). Poets learn from their favorite poets. I wonder if any of you can say that your poems are influenced by the books you've read and deal with a topic you really care about?

(See also Elizabeth Berg's two novels *Durable Goods* (1993) and *Joy School* (1997), in which young Katie is the main character. On pages 164–65 in *Durable Goods*, she talks of her poetry notebook and how she scans the alphabet to get a poem going. On pages 162–63 in *Joy School*, Katie speaks of her affection for the work of Shakespeare and her interest in writing sonnets.)

Books Noted in this Lesson

Peace Like a River Leif Enger

Durable Goods Elizabeth Berg

Joy School Elizabeth Berg

LESSON 57

Writing for Real-World Reasons

One of the reasons that we work hard on our writing is that our writing can improve the quality of our lives or the lives of people in our family or community. Whenever I stop to talk to you about the writing you are hoping to publish, I am tempted to ask, "Where do you think this writing will be two weeks from now?" That's an important question because I don't want you to write just because it is a school subject or you want to fill a portfolio or a space on a bulletin board. No, I want your writing to enter the real world—to be offered as a gift, to be used to inform others, to be shared at read-aloud time, to be performed by others, to become a family heirloom, and to be put to so many other uses.

In a novel I have just finished reading called *The Year of Pleasures* by Elizabeth Berg, a ten-year-old boy named Benny sends the following note to his new neighbor, a woman named Betta:

> My name is Benny. In case you didn't know, I live next door. Welcome to our neighborhood! If you need any help done, you can hire me. It is only fifty cents (or more if you think I did a really good job). You can call me, and here is my number, get ready it is 555-0098. Or if you don't want to do that I can be found on the block after school and on weekends. When I am done, believe me you will say Wow, Everything is perfect!!!! (2005, 47–48)

In just eight short sentences, Benny has accomplished a great deal. He has made his new neighbor feel welcome, introduced himself, sought an after-school job, provided necessary contact information, and even added some convincing detail.

I want you to know that in this writing workshop, you should feel free to use your writing time to accomplish real goals for yourselves. You may not be writing a note to a new neighbor, but you may be writing a toast for your parents' upcoming anniversary, a poster to announce a book swap at school, a letter to an editor of a newspaper, a guidebook for students who are going to visit your favorite museum, a how-to book on caring for the pets you know best, a poem for your sister's birthday, a newspaper for your block, songs to entertain your baby sister, or any other authentic writing. The workshop will become more alive if you strive to accomplish real goals with your writing.

Books Noted in this Lesson

The Year of Pleasures Elizabeth Berg

Reading List

I have placed an asterisk next to those titles that I found to be particularly brimming with passages to share with young writers. Only a small sampling of excerpts from each appears in this text.

Abraham, Pearl. 1995. *The Romance Reader.* New York: Riverhead.
Allison, Dorothy. 1992. *Bastard Out of Carolina.* New York: Penguin.
———. 1998. *Cavedweller.* New York: Penguin.
Atkinson, Kate. 1995. *Behind the Scenes at the Museum.* New York: Picador.
Azzopardi, Trezza. 2000. *The Hiding Place.* New York: Grove.
Beattie, Ann. 1989. *Picturing Will.* New York: Random House.
*Berg, Elizabeth. 1993. *Durable Goods.* New York: Random House.
———. 1997. *Joy School.* New York: Ballantine.
———. 1998. *What We Keep.* New York: Ballantine.
———. 2005. *The Year of Pleasures.* New York: Random House.
Bohjalian, Chris. 2002. *The Buffalo Soldier.* New York: Vintage.
Chai, Arlene J. 1995. *The Last Time I Saw Mother.* New York: Ballantine.
Cisneros, Sandra. 1984. *The House on Mango Street.* New York: Vintage.
Conroy, Frank. 1993. *Body and Soul.* New York: Houghton Mifflin.
Danticat, Edwidge. 1994. *Breath, Eyes, Memory.* New York: Soho.
Deane, Seamus. 1996. *Reading in the Dark.* New York: Vintage.
Devoto, Pat Cunningham. 2001. *Out of the Night That Covers Me.* New York: Warner.
Doyle, Roddy. 1993. *Paddy Clarke Ha Ha Ha.* New York: Viking.
Enger, Leif. 2001. *Peace Like a River.* New York: Grove.
Ferri, Linda. 2005. *Enchantments.* New York: Alfred A. Knopf.
Fitch, Janet. 1999. *White Oleander.* Boston: Little, Brown.

Flock, Elizabeth. 2004. *Me and Emma.* Ontario, Canada: MIRA.
Gibbons, Kaye. 1987. *Ellen Foster.* New York: Random House.
Goldberg, Myla. 2002. *Bee Season.* New York: Doubleday.
Haddon, Mark. 2004. *The Curious Incident of the Dog in the Night-Time.* New York: Vintage.
*Hamill, Pete. 1997. *Snow in August.* New York: Warner.
Hegi, Ursula. 1994. *Stones from the River.* New York: Scribner Paperback Fiction.
*Hosseini, Khaled. 2003. *The Kite Runner.* New York: Riverhead.
Jensen, Liz. 2004. *The Ninth Life of Louis Drax.* New York: Bloomsbury.
Kidd, Sue Monk. 2002. *The Secret Life of Bees.* New York: Viking.
Kincaid, Jamaica. 1983. *Annie John.* New York: Farrar, Straus and Giroux.
Kingsolver, Barbara. 1998. *The Poisonwood Bible.* New York: HarperCollins.
Lawson, Mary. 2002. *Crow Lake.* New York: Bantam Dell.
Lychack, William. 2004. *The Wasp Eater.* New York: Houghton Mifflin.
MacDonald, Ann-Marie. 2003. *The Way the Crow Flies.* New York: HarperCollins.
Maguire, Gregory. 1999. *Confessions of an Ugly Stepsister.* New York: HarperCollins.
Martel, Yann. 2001. *Life of Pi.* New York: Harcourt.
Mattison, Alice. 1995. *Hilda and Pearl.* New York: HarperCollins.
Maynard, Joyce. 2003. *The Usual Rules.* New York: St. Martin's.
McCabe, Patrick. 1993. *The Butcher Boy.* New York: Fromm International.
McDermott, Alice. 2002. *Child of My Heart.* New York: Farrar, Straus and Giroux.
McEwan, Ian. 2001. *Atonement.* New York: Anchor.
*McGhee, Alison. 2000. *Shadow Baby.* New York: Picador.
*Moriarty, Laura. 2003. *The Center of Everything.* New York: Hyperion.
Morrison, Toni. 1970. *The Bluest Eye.* New York: Pocket.
*Picoult, Jodi. 2004. *My Sister's Keeper.* New York: Atria.
Reynolds, Sheri. 1995. *The Rapture of Canaan.* New York: Berkley.
Richler, Emma. 2001. *Sister Crazy.* New York: Pantheon.
Roth, Philip. 2004. *The Plot Against America.* New York: Houghton Mifflin.
Russo, Richard. 1993. *Nobody's Fool.* New York: Random House.
Shields, Carol. 2002. *Unless.* New York: HarperCollins.
Styron, Alexandra. 2001. *All the Finest Girls.* Boston: Little, Brown.
Sullivan, Faith. 1988. *The Cape Ann.* New York: Penguin.
*Tartt, Donna. 2002. *The Little Friend.* New York: Vintage.
Toews, Miriam. 2004. *A Complicated Kindness.* New York: Counterpoint.
Wells, Rebecca. 1992. *Little Altars Everywhere.* Seattle: Broken Moon.
———. 2005. *Ya-Yas in Bloom.* New York: HarperCollins.
*Willis, Sarah. 2000. *Some Things That Stay.* New York: Farrar, Straus and Giroux.